Praise for *Autonomy-Supportive Teaching in Higher Education: A Practical Guide for College Professors*

"The question of motivation is central to any faculty member. Having a psychologist discuss the literature and AST and then provide practical, classroom-based examples of how the theory can be applied in classrooms is going to fill a pedagogical need. This book summarizes AST and the state of motivation psychology and then shows how AST works in the classroom and how faculty can apply it."
—Mark McBeth, Idaho State University

"*Autonomy-Supportive Teaching in Higher Education* examines recent scholarship on motivation in the classroom, and it offers a more nuanced approach, demonstrating how motivation is on a continuum as opposed to either extrinsic or internal."
—Melissa Vosen Callens, North Dakota State University

"A timely and practical resource, this book shares important insights into how an autonomy-supportive teaching style can bring a new perspective to understand students' motivation, enhance their learning experience, and foster well-being. Grounded in self-determination theory's decades of empirical research, the author brings autonomy-supportive teaching to life through his passion and personal experience. This book is unique and valuable as it explains in everyday language what autonomy-supportive teaching is and provides ways to implement it in practice. Highly relevant to anyone in education today."
—Scott Shelton-Strong, Kanda University of International Studies

"*Autonomy-Supportive Teaching in Higher Education: A Practical Guide for College Professors* presents faculty with a theory-based, pragmatic guide to supporting students' achievement through teaching practices that allow students to develop autonomy-based motivations and agency in completing their coursework. In the current climate of change in higher education, such an approach is attractive in its goals and methods. I found myself reading the book both as a faculty member reflecting on my own teaching as well as the director of a teaching center who can use the process and materials included in the text as the basis for impactful programming with my colleagues across campus."
—Karen Brakke, Spelman College

"To really motivate your students, you need to understand more than just the typical intrinsic/extrinsic line of thinking. This book explains how you can better support your students' autonomy for more meaningful and lasting motivation."
—Diane M. Miller, University of Houston Downtown

"Patrick Whitehead's book is an excellent guide for college instructors looking to motivate their students. It is so difficult to find a theory- and research-driven book on teaching, but Dr. Whitehead has done just that. Beside having scientific support for his methods, he also offers practical suggestions and ways to implement these ideas into any college classroom. I will be using this book in my graduate-level Teaching of Psychology course and in training future graduate teaching assistants."
—**Kristi Moore, Angelo State University; member, Texas Tech University System**

"This book presents AST in an accessible way, thus contributing to the field of teaching and learning. This is especially true as the author breaks down intrinsic motivation as an umbrella term. Understanding intrinsic motivation as a continuum rather than a fixed mindset has the potential change how instructors approach student learning."
—**Jill DeTemple, Southern Methodist University, Dedman College of Humanities and Sciences**

Autonomy-Supportive Teaching in Higher Education

A Practical Guide for College Professors

PATRICK M. WHITEHEAD
Albany State University

ROWMAN & LITTLEFIELD
Lanham • Boulder • New York • London

Executive Acquisitions Editor: Mark Kerr
Assistant Acquisitions Editor: Sarah Rinehart
Sales and Marketing Inquiries: textbooks@rowman.com

Published by Rowman & Littlefield
An imprint of The Rowman & Littlefield Publishing Group, Inc.
4501 Forbes Boulevard, Suite 200, Lanham, Maryland 20706
www.rowman.com

86-90 Paul Street, London EC2A 4NE

British Library Cataloguing in Publication Information Available

Library of Congress Cataloging-in-Publication Data

Names: Whitehead, Patrick M., 1986– author.
Title: Autonomy-supportive teaching in higher education : a practical guide
   for college professors / Patrick M. Whitehead.
Description: Lanham, Maryland : Rowman & Littlefield, [2023] | Includes
   bibliographical references and index.
Identifiers: LCCN 2022055116 (print) | LCCN 2022055117 (ebook) | ISBN
   9781538177198 (Cloth) | ISBN 9781538177204 (Paperback)
   | ISBN 9781538177211 (epub)
Subjects: LCSH: College teaching—Methodology. | College
   teaching—Psychological aspects. | Effective teaching. | Motivation in
   education. | Education, Higher—United States.
Classification: LCC LB2331 .W44 2023 (print) | LCC LB2331 (ebook) | DDC
   378.1/7—dc23/eng/20230103
LC record available at https://lccn.loc.gov/2022055116
LC ebook record available at https://lccn.loc.gov/2022055117

To Dorene Rojas Medlin,
without whom this book
would have been impossible

Brief Contents

Contents

Acknowledgments

This book would not have been possible without the support of Dr. Dorene Rojas Medlin—friend, colleague, and director of the Center for Faculty Excellence at Albany State University. Dorene listened patiently as I described my experience using autonomy-supportive teaching (AST) in my courses. She began thinking out loud about how nice it would be if other faculty tried the same thing in their courses, and how AST might make a useful contribution to existing academic programs and projects. She was supportive when I suggested that I conduct a faculty workshop, and even found a way through the center to support me financially with the project.

This book also wouldn't have happened without the suggestion from workshop participants that I do so. When conducting my original AST workshop, I was content to share previously published book chapters and articles, and then discuss the strategies for supporting autonomy in a discussion-type forum. It quickly became apparent that a more guided and structured approach would be helpful for facilitating the workshop, so I began creating sample implementation suggestions for each AST strategy. I also wrote essays to address the problems that came up during our discussions, sharing all of this with my participants. Eventually I realized that I had around 35,000 words of workshop materials, and more than one suggestion that I use the resources to write a book. So I did.

I was very encouraged by the support from Mark Kerr, education editor at Rowman & Littlefield. I enjoyed our dialog about the book, and could not believe the volume of reviews he and his colleagues obtained for my proposal. He delivered more than 30,000 words of suggestions, recommendations, criticisms, and support from college faculty and staff from all around the world.

I am grateful to the reviewers, listed here, who graciously shared their insights and concerns without any recognition. In particular, these reviews helped me understand who might find the book useful, how the book could best meet the needs of its potential readers, and what changes might result in the best finished product. They helped me understand, for example, that my casual writing style and childish drawings were not only mildly off-putting but actually seemed disrespectful to highly educated readers. Hearing variations of this concern from 30 different perspectives made an impression on me, and I made substantial changes to the manuscript. This was important feedback for me to be able to take my readers' perspective, which you will find as the first and most important strategy for supporting autonomy of others (including students). As always, any errors and omissions are my own.

Ashley G. Blackburn,	*University of Houston–Downtown*
Jerrell D. Coggburn,	*North Carolina State University*
Samir Haddad,	*Fordham University*
Tabitha Hart,	*San Jose State University*
Christine Helfrich,	*American International College*
Tamara Herold,	*University of Nevada, Las Vegas*
Katherine Hermann-Turner,	*Tennessee Tech University*
Michael Loui,	*University of Illinois Urbana–Champaign* and *Purdue University*
Cori Mathis,	*Lipscomb University*
Mark McBeth,	*Idaho State University*
Rachel Schichtl,	*University of Central Arkansas*
Daniel Sanford,	*Boise State University*
Melissa Vosen Callens,	*North Dakota State University*

Finally, I am grateful to my wife, Erica, who has put up with my irritability and stress over the past few weeks while I diligently revised, reworked, and rewrote the entire manuscript to accommodate the shifts in voice and tone that reviewers suggested.

At the recommendation of a reviewer, I tried to find a self-determination theory expert to coauthor this book. I agreed that having someone who was more deeply familiar with the field would help anchor my descriptions and examples. But, in the end, I was unable to find someone with the relevant expertise who was not too busy with existing responsibilities. Perhaps that is why a book like this has never before taken shape.

Introduction

Vignette 1: You are three weeks into teaching an online course. Everything seems to be going fine until the first major quiz deadline passes, which 40% of your students miss. You are worried, partly because the quiz is worth 10% of their final grade, but also because if this trend continues many students will fail the course. Do you

1. give your students a one-time extension of three days, but remind them that you cannot keep moving deadlines?
2. tell your students that they can complete the quiz whenever is good for them?
3. create a survey to see what time of the week is best for scheduling future deadlines for your students?
4. create a video where you celebrate the 60% of students who submitted their quiz on time along with your hope that the other 40% might become more like them?

Vignette 2: It is an evening course with graduate students and their energy level is noticeably low. Students are staring with indifference at their phones, out the window, or blankly into space. You look at your schedule for the day and see the topic is one that, in your experience, students will struggle with. Do you

1. promise that students can leave as soon as the objective of the day is met?
2. share with your students that they seem lethargic, and ask for their ideas of how best to tackle the difficult topic for the day?
3. end class right then and there, as surely it will be better to tackle the topic when students are looking more refreshed?
4. follow the course schedule as planned, careful to point out when the next major assessment will take place and how this evening's class fits into it?

Vignette 3: You are teaching a course that you have taught for years without any problems. This time, however, students seem unusually bored and apathetic. Would you say that your students' motivation

1. is missing?
2. is directed toward nonacademic outlets (e.g., social media, popular culture)?
3. has been routinely and systematically prevented?
4. is irrelevant to learning?

Each of the responses represent teaching choices that either support student autonomy and therefore boost interest, engagement, satisfaction, and enjoyment or that thwart student autonomy, leading to boredom, apathy, disinterest, and decreased psychological well-being. We will examine which choices represent which outcomes at the beginning of chapter 2. But you will be able to spot which is which well before then.

Not a Vignette

You are teaching during a period where classroom practices have become radically transformed: psychological and emotional stress have reached record highs, deaths and illnesses of family and friends have become commonplace, and normal outlets for rest and relaxation such as traveling and going out with friends have been periodically closed. College students are burned out (Salmela-Aro et al., 2022; Toubasi et al., 2022). College faculty are burned out (Garvick et al., 2022; Taylor & Frechette, 2022[1]). College staff are burned out (Loebach et al., 2020). But you already know this, of course. You are living it.

The COVID-19 pandemic has been responsible for all sorts of changes to everyday life, as well as to business, education, manufacturing, inflation, and so on. Incoming college students are dealing with these changes alongside the challenge of finding an occupational path in a disrupted and unpredictable economy.

As the author of a health psychology book, I am often asked to comment on books and articles that examine the state of healthcare, particularly from a patient-centered perspective. About six months into the pandemic, this became a once-per-week request. I received work written by scholars and researchers from all over the world who were reporting negative changes to psychological well-being among patients and providers, burnout in healthcare personnel, decreases in job satisfaction among nurses and doctors, increased stress in the workplace, increased anxiety and depression among providers, and on and on and on.

I have also seen this change directly in my wife, who works as chief medical provider in a poor rural outpatient clinic in the United States. She and her colleagues are seeing more patients who are reporting more problems than before the pandemic. Due to the rate of payment defaults, the clinics are riding along the edge of bankruptcy, with threats of layoffs always looming overhead. The impact of these loads is compounded further by the frequent and unpredictable medical leave that office managers, administration, and providers are taking due to increases in mental health problems and contraction of the coronavirus itself. None of these figures compare, however, to the now regular and heartbreaking experience of holding my defeated wife after a stressful day.

---

1. Authors found that COVID burnout affected faculty with higher teaching loads disproportionately (as compared to faculty with smaller teaching loads and greater research productivity).

In the college classroom, the changes have also been noticeable. Social distancing protocols have resulted in a bizarre hybridization and virtualization of the learning experience. Colleges and universities have scrambled to offer students college-like experiences without putting anybody at risk of infection. Faculty, at least for a time, shifted to teaching online—many of whom were forced by circumstance to do so in the middle of the spring 2020 semester. The statistics reported by Taylor and Frechette (2022)—namely, that many faculty are ill equipped and unprepared to teach online, yet they are taking on greater course loads with higher enrollments than ever before—are familiar to faculty worldwide.

Students have not been spared, either. Students who began college during fall 2020 or fall 2021 experienced an unusual conclusion to high school or secondary school. In the United States—where high school graduation is viewed as an important rite of passage—students missed the ceremony and celebrations and, instead, got to see their name printed on a list of graduates. In conversations about their junior and senior years as high schoolers, my students have reported missing entire athletic seasons, cancellation of springtime formal dances, and no end-of-school parties. Many students explained how all organized learning effectively stopped. These same students found themselves in college, where faculty were trying to figure out how to facilitate meaningful learning in their new hybrid or virtual environments.

This just happens to be where we are at this period in history. But things are looking good. On the pandemic front, at least as of fall 2022, the severity of COVID-19 seems to have abated. In the college classroom, faculty and students have learned how to make the most of digital, virtual, hybrid, and asynchronous forms of learning. In other words, we have learned what we could about our problems.

This book is a product of my own means of sorting through pandemic fatigue. It involved discovering autonomy-supportive teaching, applying it, experiencing its effects on students and myself, and then sharing what I learned with anybody who would listen. At my school, a public historically black university in the United States, this meant conducting a semester-long workshop for interested faculty.

A Revolution in My Teaching Spirit

Fall 2020 was a low point for me as a college professor. I was teaching six courses with enrollments of around 40 students per course. But there were far fewer than 40 students present each class period. By the middle of the semester, I calculated my average daily attendance to be around 25%.

I remember one of these class periods very clearly. It was a 75-student lecture course. Social distancing protocols meant that only 25 students were permitted to attend in person, but only three had shown up. They were seated in the very last row, and they were hunched over their smartphones. Another three students had logged in online to attend the course virtually, but their cameras were turned off and they were unresponsive. It was almost as if they had signed on because they felt that it was what was expected of them, even though deep down they didn't really want to. Meanwhile I felt as if I was trying to sell pagers at a mall kiosk in 2022.

For this particular class, I had taken a survey the previous week where I asked students what I could change in order to make the course better and more interesting. (I didn't know it at the time, but this was an autonomy-supportive practice.) They had responded by asking for a short introductory lecture followed by an interactive assignment. But there was a problem: none of the students who had voted during the previous week were here today. I lectured for a few minutes, but, failing to pique any student interest, I finally dropped my hands and exclaimed, "What am I supposed to do?"

The students looked up from their phones, then awkwardly at each other.

Now that I had my students' attention, I wasn't sure how to respond. So I went on to complain out loud about how helpless and discouraged I felt. I complained that none of the best teaching practices seemed to be working, and how my own intuitions and student suggestions didn't seem to be working either. I sincerely believed that I didn't know what I was doing anymore as a college professor, and my students could tell.

In the following weeks, I began looking for a job outside of academia. I looked seriously at the benefits packages of a local manufacturer. My search eventually took me to what had been my second career choice, which was to become a therapist. I had been particularly interested in a field of motivation psychology called self-determination theory (SDT), and how it had been applied in counseling psychology. I liked SDT because its practitioners recognized the importance of client autonomy, which means self-directed action. This was very different from controlling therapeutic styles in which the therapist is the expert and the client must do whatever the therapist says. SDT recognized that therapy works best when the therapist works together with the client. In the end, it is the client who does the work of getting better.

With teaching now in my rearview, I revisited the articles that I had found so interesting ten years earlier. This was a particular treat because there was another decade of research for me to catch up on. I eventually found my way to the website www.selfdeterminationtheory.org, which has tons of free resources, and I began exploring all of the ways SDT had been applied to health, meditation, sports and exercise, education, etc.

"Wait, education?" I said out loud in my study. My black lab gave me a concerned look, then went back to sleep. I hadn't realized that SDT was being applied to education.

Now, I understand that it is frowned upon to quote from a website in a book that has been written for college professors. But I also feel as though I owe it to the reader to share the lines from the website that grabbed me by the shoulders. On the landing page for SDT in education, this is what I found:

> Many teachers are in a daily struggle to energize and motivate learners who lack enthusiasm, are passive, refuse to cooperate, or even display aggressive or disruptive behaviors. [. . .] Learners' intrinsic motivation dramatically deteriorates with increasing age, and during the teenage years many learners have lost interest in and excitement for school. In this context SDT provides a sound theoretical framework that stimulates a critical perspective on some of the widely used contemporary educational policies

and practices which are hampering rather than fostering learners' intrinsic motivation. (SDT.org, 2022, np)

As silly as it feels to type it out, I genuinely felt as though the summary of SDT in education had been written for me at that crucial moment of my career. It was a rope to help me out of my pit of instructor despair.

Of course, I worried that it would never work for me as well as the website had claimed. Therefore I began downloading articles and reading them in my spare time. (Students weren't stopping by my office, so I had plenty of spare time.) I was first trying to find the data point that proved that it wouldn't work for me and my students, and only later was I trying to figure out how it worked, what it looked like, and how I might do it myself.

When SDT is applied to the classroom, the result is autonomy-supportive teaching (AST). Just as SDT counselors support the self-direction and personal growth of their clients, autonomy-supportive teachers and college professors help their students become self-directed in their learning.

The more I read, the more encouraged I felt that AST would work for me and my students. The evidence supporting AST, which I will summarize in chapter 3, is immense. It is impossible to ignore or write off.

In spring 2021, just a few months after discovering it myself, I began using what I had learned in my courses. In the weeks that followed, I found myself more excited to go to class; I noticed that I was learning a lot more about (and from) my students; I saw a greater range of emotions expressed in the classroom; there was more peer teaching, greater participation, better and more consistent attendance, and considerably more spontaneous comments of affirmation from students (e.g., "this was fun," "we kept talking about this after class," and even, "my parents have started asking me what we talked about in class each day").

If it isn't clear to the reader, then I will state it baldly: I began feeling again as though I was born to be a teacher, which for me is priceless.

I'm not alone in feeling this way after adopting the teaching strategies described in this book, either. Research indicates that teachers who adopt an autonomy-supportive style find more of what attracted them to the profession to begin with. That is to say, they (1) come to see teaching as a beloved activity, (2) find teaching to be more personally satisfying, (3) gain confidence in the classroom, and (4) feel a greater sense of purpose in their work (Cheon et al., 2020). Moreover, AST has been generalizable to all conceivable learning contexts. It has been fruitfully applied around the world; in individualist and collectivist cultures; courses in the arts, humanities, sciences, and graduate programs; in remedial courses; with students who are low income, minority, and at risk; in face-to-face, online, and asynchronous courses; and on and on.

AST Will Work for You and Your Students

All of the research I introduce in this chapter will be carefully described and discussed in chapter 3. But I don't want to make you wait until then to hear about the sorts of outcomes you can expect when you practice AST in your classrooms. To begin, I can say with confidence that AST will work for you and your students. That is, unless either of the following conditions applies to you:

1. you insist on maintaining a controlling teaching style, or
2. you have a fixed authoritarian personality.

There is a very good chance that these statements don't apply to you, because they describe a person who is not interested in professional development. Therefore, if you are interested in making a positive change in your courses, then I am confident in saying that AST will work for you.

Johnmarshall Reeve, whose books and articles have been unspeakably helpful as resources for me, provides a recent review of 51 AST interventions where teachers and college faculty were trained in AST practices (Reeve & Cheon, 2021). These studies have shown that (1) AST can be learned, (2) AST is beneficial to students, and (3) AST is beneficial to instructors. Keep in mind that these 51 studies were specifically looking at the effectiveness of the training—not the effectiveness of AST on student well-being and learning (the number of studies showing the latter would be larger by a magnitude of 10- or 20-fold). Moreover, these 51 studies represent five continents and 17 nations.

AST has been shown to be effective for students regardless of age, gender, race, nationality, and culture. Indeed, AST is particularly beneficial for nontraditional students, minority students, and students who represent other academically disadvantaged groups.

Three Potential Hurdles: Mistaken Beliefs that Interfere with Professional Development

Before undertaking any professional development activity, it is helpful to anticipate the snares that are most likely to snag you and your colleagues. I can identify three misperceptions that might interfere with a successful teaching intervention. These misperceptions are: (1) it's the students' fault, and therefore *they* are the ones who need to change; (2) you cannot teach a person how to teach, and therefore all professional development is a waste of time; and (3) that controlling teachers make the best teachers.

MISTAKEN BELIEF 1: IT'S THE STUDENTS' FAULT

In his book *For White Folks Who Teach in the Hood . . . And the Rest of Y'all, Too*, American urban educator Christopher Emdin describes a demonstration he often gives during teacher workshops. Emdin shows teachers a photograph of a boy with his head down on his desk during a high school chemistry class. He then asks teachers to explain why this is. "That's easy," teachers say, "the boy isn't interested in learning," and so on. Teachers give their version of "The student doesn't care!" as their explanation.

If a student lacks motivation, we think, then it is probably because the student is unmotivated. But we forget the role that the environment plays in facilitating a person's motivation. We forget that the motivation for learning how to balance chemical equations is nurtured by the chemistry classroom itself, as well as the years and years of science classrooms that have led up to the chemistry lessons. We forget that low student motivation is a symptom of a much deeper problem, and not the original problem itself.

In his research, Emdin had recorded hundreds of hours of classroom video footage, which he and his colleagues have analyzed. Emdin was trying to understand what was going on between teachers and their students—particularly between teachers and students in low income and minority schools, like the ones Emdin had attended as a student in the Bronx section of New York City, USA. This meant that the photograph of the boy was actually a still frame from a video. After the teachers had given their explanations during the demonstration, Emdin rewound the tape a full minute. As the tape is rewinding, the audience of finger-wagging teachers sees the boy's head up off the desk and bouncing around between flailing arms. The animation is most unexpected. It hardly screams "unmotivated." When the tape is played back, the teachers watch in amazement as the boy tries to answer his teacher's question at least seven times. There was a lot of chatter in the classroom, and we cannot see what the teacher is doing. But we can hear the teacher continue to ask his question, even though there is a boy in the middle of the room with his hands on his head shouting the answer over and over in exasperation. In the end, the teacher concludes that nobody can solve the problem, and he announces the answer to the class. Only then does the boy's head hit his desk.

When asked a second time about the boy's problem, the teachers give a very different answer.

I had a chance to meet Emdin after he gave an honorarium lecture at my university. I had read about this demonstration, and I asked him if he still had the video footage of the boy in the chemistry class. I was hoping that he might email me a YouTube link at a later time, but he pulled his laptop out in the middle of his lunch (yes, I interrupted his lunch), and he searched until he found it. We watched it together as the boy repeatedly tried to get his teacher's attention. Emdin enthusiastically pointed and counted out loud each time the boy gave the correct answer.

Emdin's enthusiasm was inspired by this boy's persistence. It was the wave of pride and satisfaction that a teacher gets whenever they witness a student turn on to the teacher's subject matter. As the excitement disappeared from the boy's voice and actions, we began to feel his frustration. Eventually the boy's head went down in defeat. It was hard not to feel that defeat myself. Emdin, of course, got fired up. It was clear that he had to tell this boy's story, and the stories of all the other kids and college students who are ignored or who remain unseen in the classroom. That's what he focuses on in his books.

The boy in the demonstration didn't need to be motivated. He didn't need to be coaxed or coerced into giving a chemistry performance. The boy was already eager to participate with his teacher in solving the problem. He wanted to confront the challenge and demonstrate his skill. But he wasn't supported by his teacher in any of these actions, so he eventually gave up. Disinterest in learning is a consequence of learning environments that fail to support students' basic psychological needs.

The teaching strategies that Emdin calls for overlap AST to a considerable degree. This overlap is discussed in chapter 3.

MISTAKEN BELIEF 2: TEACHERS CANNOT CHANGE

The second belief is that teachers—and tenured college professors in particular—cannot change. If they have learned to give lectures and exams, then that is all that they could be expected to do.

But instructors *can* change. The evidence is clear on this. In chapter 3, I report statistics on over 50 teacher-training courses where K–12 and college professors from all over the world successfully integrated AST into their classrooms.

The belief that college professors cannot change is linked to what American psychologist Carol Dweck (2006) calls a fixed mindset. When people have a fixed mindset, they believe that they are the way that they are, and nothing can change that. People with fixed mindsets don't like practicing skills that they are not already good at, and they tend to avoid challenges. A fixed mindset may be contrasted with growth mindset, which is where a person understands that their skills and capabilities can improve if they are systematically practiced. Growth mindset individuals enjoy being challenged, because they know that growth occurs as a consequence of facing challenges.

The best part of Dweck's theory is that mindsets can be changed. In her book, she talks about how to cultivate a growth mindset in children and in students.

As you might imagine, fixed mindset college faculty avoid professional development opportunities. They are reluctant to reflect on their work inside the classroom, and they are resistant to any sort of feedback or evaluation that might challenge or threaten their fixed identity. Dweck's theory will be discussed further in its relation to AST shortly.

MISTAKEN BELIEF 3: CONTROLLING TEACHERS ARE THE BEST TEACHERS

There is an unfortunate irony at the heart of what we believe makes someone a good or bad teacher. People, particularly those in the United States, think that controlling teachers are the best teachers, even though evidence suggests that they're not.

Drawing on dozens of studies conducted using K–12 and higher education classrooms, Reeve (2009) observes this mistaken belief. He writes,

> Given that students relatively benefit when teachers support their autonomy but relatively suffer when teachers control their behavior, one might expect that teachers would commonly enact autonomy-supportive instructional behaviors and only rarely enact controlling ones. This does not, however, seem to be the case. (p. 159)

To explain the persistence of this false belief, Reeve turns to the cultures that have produced it. "The U.S. culture generally evaluates teachers who use controlling instructional strategies as more competent than teachers who use autonomy-supportive strategies"

(p. 165). This belief continues despite evidence that students in controlling classrooms perform worse on common standards than students in autonomy-supportive classrooms.

In a controlling classroom, teachers pressure their students to think, feel, and act in a teacher-prescribed way. Controlling teachers neglect their students' perspectives, calling them "silly" or "uninformed" or "stupid" or "naïve" and on and on. Controlling teachers are impatient with their students, and dismiss negative feelings as unhelpful or quarrelsome. Controlling teachers do the majority of the talking.

These features in a controlling classroom combine to diminish students' inner motivation, which leads to resistance from students who are defending themselves from existential annihilation. Existential annihilation may sound strong, but what else would you call abandoning autonomy, will, and desire? Resistance comes in the forms of amotivation (e.g., giving up) and confrontation (e.g., pushing back).

Seeing and feeling resistance in the classroom, controlling teachers become more controlling. Students react by becoming more withdrawn. The cycle continues until steam is pouring out of teachers' ears and students are lifeless and unfeeling. This cycle is modeled in figure 0.1. Controlling teachers do not need to represent the drill sergeant in figure 0.1 in order to be controlling. Controlling teaching can also rely on student guilt, and might look like the fourth instructor response to vignette 1.

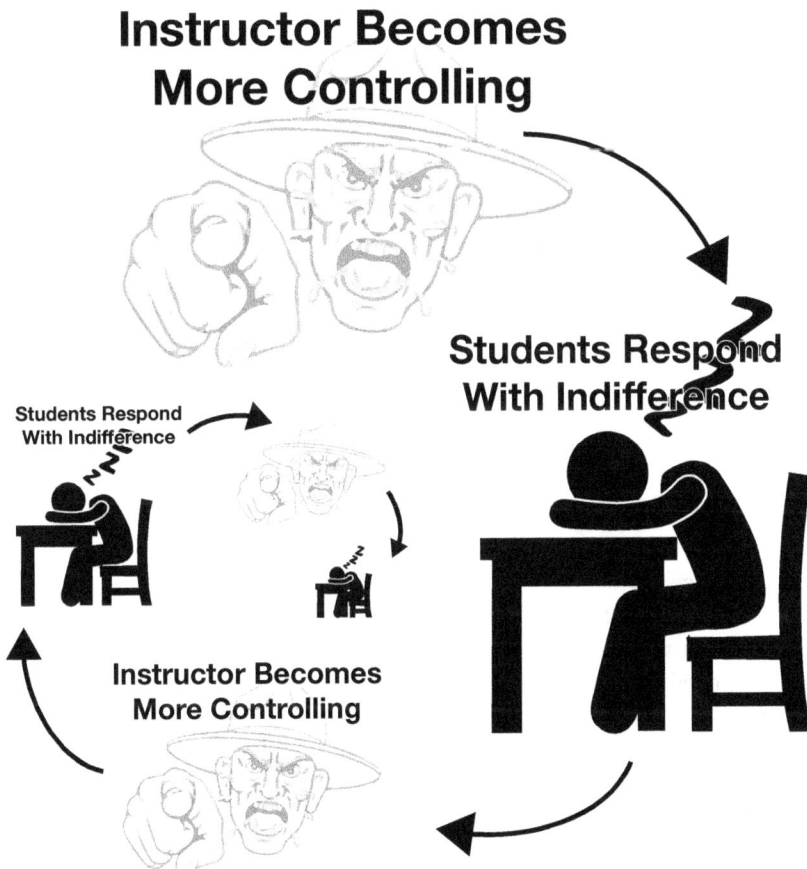

Instructor Becomes More Controlling

Students Respond With Indifference

Students Respond With Indifference

Instructor Becomes More Controlling

Figure 0.1. Cycle of controlling teaching and student motivation

Administrators play a role in this cycle of control, too, and controlling administrators have been found to result in more controlling teachers and less motivated students (Reeve, 2009).

In this demotivation cycle, the students give up on participating in their learning, and the teachers give up on facilitating it. This is a teaching nightmare, and I think it is responsible for the burnout that I had experienced when my passion for teaching had dried up. But there is good news: the demotivation cycle can be stopped.

The cycle can also work in the reverse. When students perceive that their autonomy is being supported by their instructor, they experience greater psychological well-being, greater interest and curiosity, and they engage more deeply and completely in their courses. The subsequent bubbling of student creativity, insight, and enchantment is encouraging to the instructor, who then doubles down on their support of student autonomy. The instructor, with care, begins trusting students with more and more of the learning process.

It should be noted that controlling teaching and autonomy-supportive teaching are not opposites. That is to say, a teacher could abandon control without becoming autonomy supportive. An example of this would be a classroom where students do whatever they want without rhythm or structure or feedback or any attention at all from the teacher. In this example, the students do not have the experience of being supported. What they experience is abandonment, which has been called a laissez-faire teaching style (Aelterman et al., 2019). To avoid replacing control with indifference or absence, teachers are encouraged to use structure. This will all be discussed in more detail in chapter 2.

Relation to Other Psychologies of Student Motivation

SDT is not the only motivation theory that has been applied in the classroom. In this section, I look at three common motivational approaches and explore how they overlap with SDT and its application in AST.

GRIT: PASSION AND DETERMINATION WITH ANGELA DUCKWORTH AND CAL NEWPORT

Psychologist Angela Duckworth was not interested in what makes the top 10% of people rise to the top 10%. She was interested in the top 1%. She sought out the top handful of students at the top universities in the United States, and she interviewed them. She also interviewed highly successful CEOs, musicians, athletes, and performers—always trying to understand what it was about their personalities, practices, and habits that got them to the top of their fields. She learned that all of them scored highly in two factors: passion and perseverance. By passion, Duckworth meant that these individuals were strongly driven by inner direction. By perseverance, Duckworth meant that these individuals stuck with a skill or project without wavering for many, many years. Duckworth called this fierce combination of motivational traits "grit" (2016).

It is easy to imagine how a person with an inborn passion for rock climbing would persevere long enough through disciplined training to become a fantastic rock climber. That is to say, it is easy to assume that grit is primarily driven by passion. But that isn't the case. Duckworth maintained that passion could be grown. The more a person devoted themselves to a disciplined and systematic practice of a skill, the greater their passion became. It is not passion that drives persistence. It was the other way around: persistence drives passion.

This detail was also picked up by MIT physics professor Cal Newport in his book *So Good They Can't Ignore You: Why Skills Trump Passion in the Quest for Work You Love* (2012). Newport provides a series of case studies that demonstrate Duckworth's thesis—namely, that highly successful people develop passion for their work by spending loads of time devoted to that work.

For higher education, this means that when students (and faculty) work hard at a skill, they will develop a passion for that skill. A student doesn't enjoy writing? By systematically practicing word choice, writing technique, and grammar, students will begin to enjoy the writing process more and find it more fulfilling. A professor doesn't like taking their students' points of view? By systematically working on this perspective taking, the professor will get better at it *and* find it to be a fulfilling and worthwhile practice.

AST benefits directly from the findings of Duckworth and Newport. The process of growing passion for an activity or skill can be compared to the SDT process of internalization, which is where something done for extrinsic reasons (such as a grade) will eventually be done for personal reasons (such as because it is what the student enjoys). The process of internalization will be discussed in detail in chapter 1.

FIXED AND GROWTH MINDSETS WITH CAROL DWECK

Psychologist Carol Dweck was wondering why some students became easily frustrated and would shut down when faced with a challenge while others get excited—almost as though they were energized by the difficulty. As she explored this question more deeply, Dweck began to see this binary everywhere: When given the choice, some people will err on the side of simplicity while others sought complexity; some people favored ease while others favored difficulty; some people preferred compliments while others preferred criticism; and so on. It was almost as if some people are born to grow, develop, and achieve while others were born to merely skirt by.

Dweck did what any scientist would do when confronted with a repeated finding. She created two categories—one for the people who shied away from challenges, and another for the people who sought out challenges and thrived in their midst. Then she began asking each group the same set of questions. Questions such as, "Do you feel smart only when you perform a skill flawlessly, or when you make a mistake?"

Each group answered this question differently. The group that ignored problems and avoided problems felt smart when they could perform a skill flawlessly. What Dweck realized was that this group believed that intelligence was something that was fixed in each person. They believed that mistakes were indications that a person was not intelligent. Dweck explained that this group had a fixed mindset.

The other group—the ones who got excited by challenges—believed that intelligence was fluid, and that mistakes were a great way to learn and grow and to therefore build higher intelligence. Dweck referred to this group as having a growth mindset.

In the classroom, fixed mindset students are anxious about assessments, final grades, and any tests of achievement or ability. They are unlikely to listen to critical feedback or suggestions from their teachers or fellow classmates. In their ideal scenario, fixed mindset students wish to graduate as exactly the same person they were when they started. Fixed mindset students are interested in doing only what is expected of them and nothing more, because anything more is simply asking for more attention, and this attention may expose a hidden weakness.

Growth mindset students, by comparison, are excited about assessments and final grades in order to demonstrate what they have learned and identify their weaknesses. They are the first students to ask for feedback on their work, and they take this feedback as evidence that there is always room for improvement. Growth mindset students are more likely to internalize the learning objectives, by which I mean they are more likely to adopt course goals as their own goals in order to help them become a better and more capable student or scholar.

The good news, Dweck tells us, is that mindset can be changed. A person with a fixed mindset can be nurtured and guided in such a way that they begin to recognize their capacity for growth. For example, if a student fails a written exam and feels as if their world has ended, the instructor can focus on the reality that the exam score indicates room for specific improvement. That is to say, the score can be shown to indicate the pathway forward, and not the final judgment on this student's writing ability.

Similarly, an instructor could encourage students to adopt a fixed mindset. They might do this by indicating that grades represent student capability, or by making comments such, "Some people just weren't born to be successful at physics."

In my opinion, growth mindsets would likely be facilitated by autonomy support, and fixed mindsets facilitated by control. However, I do think that Dweck's specific examples of how to facilitate a growth mindset using guided reflection questions with students adds something more than what AST accomplishes. I see autonomy support and growth mindset support to be mutually beneficial. This perspective is partially supported by a study conducted on 1,741 adolescent children in China (Ma et al., 2022). Researchers found the highest and most optimal level of emotional regulation in students whose instructors had been autonomy supportive. With female students, this regulation was even higher when instructors were autonomy supportive *and* facilitated a growth mindset. The AST–growth mindset relationship was not found with the male students.

More research examining the relationship between mindset and autonomy support would be helpful to all instructors who are interested in supporting their students' long-term growth and psychological well-being.

WHY WE LEARN THE WAYS THAT WE LEARN WITH JOSH EYLER

The book you hold in your hands provides plenty of evidence that AST can be applied to the college classroom to the benefit of students and instructors alike. This evidence also fits into a theory (i.e., SDT) that is useful for predicting how and explaining why it works. In other words, AST belongs to its own scientific system for understanding human emotion. It is complete.

But you might still be wondering why practicing patience and acknowledging students' negative feelings leads to increased scores on tests of achievement, or why taking students' perspective helps those students become better writers or more skilled at algebra and calculus. These questions will inevitably lead you beyond the field of the psychology of motivation and into fields such as anthropology, cognitive science and neuroscience, evolutionary biology, and even history and the humanities. This is precisely what humanities professor Josh Eyler accomplishes in his book *How Humans Learn: The Science and Stories Behind Effective College Teaching* (2018).

Eyler explores each of these disciplines and traces their relationship to each other and how they meet inside the classroom where learning is going on. He describes curiosity, sociality, emotion, authenticity, and failure—each from the perspective of the intersecting disciplines as well as from what is going on in the classroom. For example, in the chapter on curiosity, which he admits is a difficult concept to nail down, Eyler explains how neuroscientists have demonstrated how humans are driven by the experience of novelty. Novel experiences result in a release of the neurotransmitter dopamine, which is associated with feelings of pleasure. This helps us understand why it is fun to explore new topics. But Eyler takes this further by adding a layer of evolutionary biology. He compares homo sapiens to our closest relatives, primates, and shares evidence about how, despite sharing over 98% of DNA, homo sapiens demonstrate curiosity whereas primates do not. In other words, curiosity is a uniquely human phenomenon.

I won't give it all away here, but I do hope to demonstrate the kinds of insights that Eyler provides instructors of all levels in his book. He closes each chapter with a handful of concrete examples of what the learning element looks like in the classroom and how it might be facilitated. These are intended as illustrations, and not necessarily as guides to be followed.

Eyler helps us understand that the strategies that seem to work in the classroom are not mere products of the past 50 years. They have been in progress for millennia. In sum, Eyler shares the narrative for why we learn the ways that we learn; the book you are holding is a guide for facilitating learning. There are clear points of overlap, but even here the overlap is such that Eyler provides a cross disciplinary perspective of what, for example, relatedness means for classroom learning.

Structure of This Book

I have been careful to design this book around the three steps that experts recommend for training AST practitioners (Aelterman et al., 2013; Reeve & Cheon, 2021). That way it will be useful as a resource for organizing faculty workshops, learning communities, and professional development courses. These steps are:

1. A Theoretical Background of AST
2. An Overview of the AST Strategies
3. Exercises for Application

In part I (chapters 1, 2, and 3), I introduce the theory of autonomy-supportive teaching. Chapter 1 introduces SDT from which AST stems. Here I focus primarily on the mini SDT theory of internalization, which is the process by which an external belief, value, or behavior (such as a course learning objective) is accepted and adopted by students wholeheartedly. Chapter 2 introduces AST more specifically, and begins with a discussion of the vignettes that opened this introduction.

Chapter 3 is a review chapter. In it I summarize the evidence that AST works in the classroom. I focus exclusively on its usefulness in colleges, universities, and graduate programs. I also explore evidence that AST is especially helpful for nontraditional students, minority and underrepresented students, and students with poor academic preparation.

Part II (chapters 4–8) provides the workshops. Chapter 4 focuses on SDT, and it begins with practices aimed at familiarizing faculty with the themes of emotional regulation, psychological well-being, psychological need satisfaction, autonomy support, and control.

Chapter 5 introduces the assessment tools for diagnosing teaching styles. These self-report tools adopt the instructor's perspective, the students' perspective, and a classroom visitor's perspective. I discuss how to use these tools to anticipate the sorts of changes you might expect to find in your own classrooms after implementing the AST strategies.

The chapter 6 workshop is designed to help faculty adopt the first AST strategy, which is "Taking Students' Perspective." Because this step is integral to all of the strategies that follow, extra time will be spent on examples and activities.

Chapter 7 is a workshop about supporting students' intrinsic motivation, which includes AST strategy 2, "Inviting Students to Pursue Their Interests," and AST strategy 3, "Present Learning Activities in Need-Satisfying Ways." These will be presented through description, examples, and activities for application.

Chapter 8 is a workshop that introduces faculty to the remaining AST strategies— strategy 4, "Providing Explanatory Rationale"; strategy 5, "Acknowledging Negative Feelings"; strategy 6, "Relying on Invitational Language"; and strategy 7, "Displaying Patience." Once again, each strategy will be introduced through description, examples, and activities for application.

Part III is for putting finishing touches on the implementation of AST, and for troubleshooting any problems that emerge. In chapter 9, I provide a sample self-study of the impact that AST had on a pair of online courses that I taught over a summer term. This is shared as an example of how an AST program might be evaluated after its implementation, as well as to provide an example of how AST might be used in online courses. In chapter 10, I look carefully at some of the more subtle changes that have occurred in my own perspective about teaching and learning since I began practicing AST.

In the conclusion, I summarize the problems that occurred for me and my colleagues during our workshop. This is provided to help instructors anticipate and troubleshoot problems as they occur. I also invite interested readers and future AST practitioners to document the impact that the practice has had on their students, courses, programs, departments, and so on. While the research support for AST in higher education is vast, there is still a great deal of room for improvement. In particular, I argue that we need more research and examples of how to support student autonomy in online courses.

Part I

THEORY

CHAPTER 1

Self-Determination Theory and Higher Education

In the hallway outside the faculty offices one afternoon, a colleague shared her frustration over trying to get her students to read *Macbeth*. The situation was especially troubling because *Macbeth* was her favorite play. She was heartbroken and confused by her students' indifference. I could feel her disappointment.

Inside, my colleague was a rubber band ball of conflicting best teaching practices. She was convinced, for example, that she was supposed to let her students read whatever they wanted. That's the only way for them to actualize their true learning potential, right? But then she also knew that she was supposed to penalize students who didn't do the reading, because students needed to learn that there are consequences to their actions. How else would they learn? Or maybe this was one of those cases where she needed to integrate TikTok and YouTube videos into the reading assignments in order to spice them up.

Student motivation lies at the center of each of these strategies, but it is hard to decide which motivational strategy to use with which learning activity. This difficulty is compounded when the instructors themselves are beginning to feel the same sort of indifference and apathy that their students are exhibiting.

College instructors now have over 100 years of motivation research to consult when designing courses and classroom activities. As I am writing this, more research is being done about how to best facilitate significant and meaningful learning experiences. Every new generation of motivational theory has believed its approach to be the final solution to education. To demonstrate this, I will discuss three of these theories: behaviorism, in which it is understood that human actions are ruled by external forces (i.e., extrinsic motivation); humanism, in which it is understood that human actions are ruled by internal forces (i.e., intrinsic motivation); and self-determination theory, in which human actions are understood to be ruled by external *and* internal forces, and in which it is possible to facilitate a shift from one to the other (i.e., internalization).

A Brief History of the Psychology of Student Motivation

William James explored motivational concepts such as will and volition in his *Principles of Psychology* more than 130 years ago, but the first systematic examination of motivation occurred in the laboratories of the American behavioral psychologists, notably Edward Thorndike (1910), John Watson (1930), and B. F. Skinner (1958, 1971). The behaviorists believed that they could use behavioral science to make any student become anything.

The behaviorist theory of motivation begins with the belief that humans are born in a completely neutral way. Each new human life is as pure and as unassuming as a fresh blanket of snow. Behaviorists believed that humans developed their rich and widely diverse personalities and opinions based only on the experiences they have had and the environments that have surrounded them. This means that, from the very first moments of an infant's life, the environment and the people in it are the infant's teachers.

The implications of the behaviorist theory in education are striking. Watson, for example, believed that student engagement could be scientifically controlled. He famously claimed that he could shape any infant into becoming any sort of professional he desired. "Give me a dozen healthy infants," he said, "and I'll guarantee to take any one of them at random and train him to become any type of specialist I might select—doctor, lawyer, artist" (1930, p. 104).

Behaviorists believed that human behavior could be modified by controlling its consequences. If the consequence was favorable, then the behavior that preceded it would be repeated. If the consequence was unfavorable, then the behavior would not be repeated (or go into hiding). This conditioning practice is still pervasive in higher education today. Here are a few examples of what it looks like in a typical college classroom:

- *Students who show up more than three minutes late to class will be marked absent* (punishment)
- *If you attend the suicide prevention workshop, then I will give you 10 extra credit points* (reinforcement)
- *Students with perfect attendance do not have to take the final exam* (negative reinforcement)
- *Excuse me! If you have something to say, then you will indicate this by raising your hand* (punishment)
- *I will periodically give pop quizzes to see if you have done the reading* (random reinforcement schedule)
- *Students who do well will receive an A grade* (reinforcement)
- *Students who do poorly will receive an F grade* (punishment)

The behaviorist theory is attractive because it is entirely empirical and objective. You and I can identify and control an independent variable (such as when and how to assign work to students), and then we can look for and measure an independent variable (such as how quickly or accurately students complete that work). These forces are not hidden inside of students. Everything is out in the open.

In the 1940s and 1950s in the United States (and shortly thereafter in Europe), another theory began to emerge. This was Kurt Goldstein's motivational theory of self-actualization (Goldstein, 1934/1995; Maslow, 1943; Whitehead, 2016). For Goldstein and Abraham Maslow—the psychologist whom Goldstein inspired—humans are primarily driven by an inner force to actualize their unique potential. External motivators such as food and safety are important, but, once these basic survival needs are satisfied, humanistic psychologists believed that humans were motivated from within.

One of the best examples of this self-actualizing process that I have found comes from the story of Austrian psychiatrist Viktor Frankl (in his memoir, *Man's Search for Meaning*). Frankl survived the most notorious Nazi death camps, watching as nearly every other prisoner he met was executed or died of starvation. As World War II was coming to an end and the Nazi defenses were weakening, Frankl had an opportunity to escape. He confronted the unmistakable push of survival instinct, but he did not flee. Instead, Frankl stayed inside the camp walls in order to tend to a fellow prisoner who needed medical attention. His need to self-actualize was greater than his need to survive. Like many college professors who feel called to the education and mentorship of young people, Frankl-the-physician felt called to be a healer to those in physical distress. For Frankl, there was a motivational power that was more important than survival. (In a dramatic twist, this also saved his life.)

Frankl called this something more "personal meaning"—that is, a fire that burns inside that allows the human to persist in even the most inhospitable and brutal of environments. For years in the camps, Frankl watched what happened as this fire died in his fellow prisoners. He could see it in their eyes and in their behaviors. Their indifference would grow. They would stop eating. If the malnourishment didn't kill them, then they would eventually stop getting up. When their will to personal meaning had dried up, the body would soon follow.

Existential and humanistic psychologists, including Frankl himself, spent many decades trying to clarify this inner motivational quality. They struggled, however, to get beyond tentative explanations for how this inner motivation could lead to personal growth and development. Frankl, who reasoned that the inner drive sprang from a single life purpose, would ask his clients and college students a series of deeply personal questions about the meaning and significance of their lives. For those who had little or no recognizable inner purpose, Frankl recommended volunteer work. Maslow interviewed students about their most memorable and positive experiences, and he used their responses to describe the phenomenological structure of self-actualization and peak experiences. He differentiated between being needs and deficiency needs, but these definitions remained ambiguous, and it was difficult to apply to the classroom in any methodical way.

The strong draw that humanistic psychology has had is testament to the belief in the importance of inner and intrinsic motivations. But the failure to develop systematic procedures for research and application around the theory kept it from growing and spreading. Some scholars have speculated that it was this failure that was responsible for the floundering of humanistic psychology (Cain, 2003; Elkins, 2008).

Humanistic therapist and educator Carl Rogers was unique in that he maintained a rigorous research program where he applied what he called the principles of any help-ing relationship (which were congruence, unconditional positive regard, and empathy) to therapy (1961), peer mediation (1995), and teaching (1969, 1984). Rogers believed that facilitators (i.e., therapists or college professors) could reliably nurture the growth of inner direction and inner motivation in clients and students. In the classroom, these methods continued to be applied and tested into the twenty-first century (Rogers et al., 2014). Rogers called for a style of teacher training that very much resembled group therapy, and he was criticized for this (Jones, 1999; Milton, 2002). Perhaps this was why his methods for teaching never replaced the behaviorist paradigm that still domi-nated learning theory into the 1960s and 1970s.

But newer theories of human motivation were only just beginning. These theories benefited from the development of cognitive psychology, which applied the experimental rigor of behaviorism to psychological processes that are unseen (such as thinking, feeling, problem solving, and so on; Baars, 1986). Psychologists were beginning to realize that the relationship between environment and behavior was more sophisticated and nuanced than a simple A→B relationship (see, e.g., Breland & Breland, 1961; Seligman, 1991).

For example, take a look at what was happening in the classroom: psychologists were finding that when teachers gave their students rewards for completing assignments, the students responded with increased indifference toward the assigned activity. The students also spent less time working, they were more likely to cheat or skip parts of it, they were less likely to complete it, and they were less likely to work on the assignment in their free time (Deci & Flaste, 1995; Kohn, 2018; Ryan & Deci, 2017). Looking only at the external environment, in which goodies had been promised to students for doing their work, these results were confusing. Internal factors were evidently at play. Thankfully, the research methods of cognitive psychology had developed enough that psychologists could test these internal and unseen processes using randomized control trials. As they began doing so, a new picture of human motivation began to take form.

Almost as if picking up where Goldstein, Maslow, and Frankl had left off in their speculation about inner motivational processes, psychologists in the 1970s and 1980s were identifying and clarifying those inner processes. Just like humans' physical needs for survival could be named (e.g., food, water, shelter), so too could we identify and clarify humans' psychological needs for flourishing. Psychologists, notably Edward Deci and Richard Ryan (2017), named this new field of research after what their research had yielded, which was the understanding that humans are motivated by self-determined action. That is to say, humans are happiest when they are autonomous. They called this new field of human motivation "self-determination theory."

Self-Determination Theory and the Three Basic Psychological Needs

Over the past four decades, self-determination theory scholars and researchers have identified three basic psychological needs that, when satisfied, "facilitate growth, integrity and well-being" (Ryan & Deci, 2017, p. 82). If any of these basic needs are frustrated, then there are "serious psychological harms" (p. 82).

Maslow, in his theory of motivation, also suggests that there are at least three psychological needs beyond the basic needs of survival (these are love, self-esteem, and self-actualization), which he has arranged into a hierarchy. Maslow's model, however, is a difficult one to follow. Maslow himself lists seven exceptions to the hierarchical relationship, and he admits that the details of how or why these needs are satisfied remain unclear. That is to say, the predictive capability of Maslow's (1943) theory of motivation is limited by the following factors: the role of unconscious motivations, cultural differences, impact of partial need satisfaction, and multiple and competing motivations, among others (pp. 389–391).

In comparison, the three basic psychological needs defined by self-determination theory are attractively concise, as well as internationally and interculturally robust.

In their comprehensive overview of self-determination theory, Ryan and Deci (2017) have explained the conditions that must be met in order for a psychological state to qualify as a basic psychological need. For example, it should be "associated with seeking out or preferring certain types of experiences and with feeling good and thriving when those basic experiences are obtained" (p. 85). It must also satisfy the following nine standards for identifying a basic psychological need (as identified by Baumeister & Leary, 1995):

1. Satisfaction of the need should produce positive effects readily under all but adverse conditions.
2. Its satisfaction should have affective consequences.
3. The need should direct cognitive processing.
4. Thwarting the need should lead to negative effects on health or well-being.
5. The need should elicit or organize goal-oriented behaviors designed to satisfy them.
6. The need should be universal (i.e., it should apply across nations and cultures).
7. The need should not be derivative of other motives.
8. The need should have an impact across a broad array of behaviors.
9. The need has implications beyond immediate psychological functioning. (Adapted from Ryan & Deci, 2017, p. 85)

As you might expect, there cannot be too many perceived needs that satisfy all of these conditions. Indeed, there are only three: the need for autonomy, the need for competence, and the need for relatedness.

AUTONOMY

"The need for autonomy," Ryan and Deci (2017) explain, "describes the need of individuals to experience self-endorsement and ownership of their actions—to be self-regulating in the technical sense of that term" (p. 86). They are careful to clarify that autonomy is not to be confused or conflated with independence. This is because it is possible to be autonomous while choosing to depend on another person, or to prefer an activity where you are directed by somebody else. When assembling a piece of furniture or preparing a recipe, for example, I sometimes prefer to follow rigid instructions rather than follow my intuition. I can do so without losing my autonomy.

For college faculty, examples of autonomy might include

- choosing course materials,
- designing a weekly schedule of courses,
- joining a professional or research association,
- volunteering to join a college committee, or
- choosing what to wear and how to present themselves.

"The opposite of autonomy," Ryan and Deci continue, "is heteronomy, as when one acts out of internal or external pressures that are experienced as controlling" (p. 86).

For college faculty, the experience of control might include

- being assigned a textbook,
- taking an assigned teaching schedule,
- pressure to join a specific research association,
- assignment to a college committee, or
- following a dress code.

In these lists, I have intentionally used identical behaviors in order to demonstrate how difficult it is to tease autonomy from control by looking only at behavior. Notice also how it would be possible to practice autonomy by asking for guidance on any of these decisions. For example, "I am having trouble choosing a textbook for human development; do you have any suggestions?" Or, "I would like to participate a little bit more in the department; are there any committees that I could join?"

COMPETENCE

Another basic psychological need is for competence. "Competence refers to feeling effective in one's interactions with the social environment—that is, experiencing opportunities and supports for the exercise, expansion, and expression of one's capacities and talents" (Ryan & Deci, 2017, p. 86). I feel competent whenever I change the oil in my car without it spilling all over the driveway, and without the job resulting in total engine failure. In the classroom, I feel competent when the computer turns on and swiftly connects to the internet.

For students, competence might include any of the following:

- The ability to effectively use a new vocabulary term
- The memory of a specialized bit of knowledge
- The awareness of multiple solutions to a single problem
- The ability to design a study in order to test a hypothesis
- The ability to express their position with respect to a topic

Competence is not unlike late American developmental psychologist Erik Erikson's concept of industry, which refers to the capability a person experiences when they effect change in their environment or in other people (Erikson, 1994). For Erikson, the stifling or thwarting of industry in children or in adults results in the feeling of inferiority—that is, a person feeling as though they are better off not even trying.

The opposite of competence is failure to grasp, understand, or demonstrate something as it is being learned. This can occur if a learning activity is too difficult for the ability level of students. It is also possible, however, for students to feel unchallenged and therefore feel unable to demonstrate their competence completely (Clifford, 1990).

RELATEDNESS

The final basic psychological need is relatedness, which is "feeling connected and involved with others and having a sense of belonging" (Ryan & Deci, 2017, p. 86). The opposite of relatedness is the feeling of isolation or loneliness.

In the classroom, relatedness might look like any of the following:

- Students work together toward a common goal
- Students recognize similarities between themselves and other students, or they feel their differences taken into consideration and honored
- Students feel listened to and heard by their instructors, and they see the impact of their actions on the classroom activities
- Course materials and guest speakers represent students' backgrounds and interests

SUPPORTING BASIC PSYCHOLOGICAL NEEDS

As I described in the introduction, I learned about SDT through its application to counseling and psychotherapy. With therapy, SDT provides an entire framework for mental health disorders and their treatment. Mood disorders and other psychological disturbances are understood to stem in part from the stifling of basic psychological needs. A person loses interest and pleasure in daily tasks that stifle opportunities for autonomy, that are unchallenging, or that require the person to become alienated from others. SDT therapists work with clients to recognize opportunities for self-direction, even finding small pockets of the day where autonomy can be practiced. Ryan and Deci (2017) explain,

> We theorize that, when any of these three basic psychological needs is frustrated or neglected either in a given domain or in general, the individual will show motivational, cognitive, affective, and other psychological decrements of a specifiable nature, such as lowered vitality, loss of volition, greater fragmentation, and diminished well-being. Thus general need support will predict general vitality and well-being, but we can also look at need support within specific contexts, such as a classroom, a workplace, or an athletic team, expecting that basic need satisfactions versus frustrations will affect context-specific functioning and experience. (p. 86)

WHY THE STUDENTS WOULDN'T READ *MACBETH*

If educators are looking only at the external environment when trying to understand motivation, then they will miss the role played by the satisfaction or frustration of students' basic psychological needs. Rewarding a student for showing up on time or giving the correct answer may be pleasurable to the student (and thus satisfy part of the requirement of a basic universal need), but doing so does not result in student flourishing. Therefore rewards do not meet all nine criteria of a universal basic need. Indeed, grades and other goodies for academic performance smother student interest, self-direction, and psychological well-being. This is why professors Covington, von Hoene, and Voge (2017) have argued that we college faculty move beyond grades if we are interested in supporting intrinsic motivation and the flourishing of our students. In their estimation, grades kill intrinsic motivation.

After examining the research, it is easy to understand student apathy. Why don't students want to read *Macbeth*? Here's the answer: ever since before they could walk, these young adults have been conditioned to think of learning as nothing more than a ticket to an ice cream cone or pizza party. At some point the learner reaches a point of diminishing returns where they will ponder, "Perhaps six hours spent reading a difficult play is not worth the free ice cream cone." Teacher and writer Alfie Kohn (2018) summarizes nicely this predicament in his aptly titled book *Punished by Rewards: The Trouble with Gold Stars, Incentives, A's, Praise, and Other Bribes.*

The Many Forms of Extrinsic Motivation

As you are beginning to realize, the traditional external motivators that instructors have at their disposal (e.g., grades, smiley faces, and so on) do the opposite of what we have long hoped: they have a negative impact on student psychological need satisfaction and well-being. This occurs even though students report nothing more desirable than receipt of an A at the end of the semester.

What, then, are college professors to do? Course learning objectives often come from departments, colleges, distant regents or chancellors, and even accrediting agencies. Objectives seldom come from the students themselves. Thankfully, just because an objective is coming from outside the students doesn't mean that it cannot be presented in a way that facilitates students' inner motivational processes. In other words, an extrinsic goal (such as reading comprehension) can be taught in a way that it supports students' basic psychological needs, and is therefore adopted as though it was the students' goal all along (i.e., it becomes internalized). Ryan and Deci (2000) explain, "SDT recognizes that extrinsically motivated actions can also become self-determined as individuals identify with and fully assimilate their regulation. Thus, it is through internalization and integration that individuals can be extrinsically motivated and still be committed and authentic" (p. 74).

Whenever I present autonomy supportive teaching to educators, nearly everybody recognizes an emphasis on intrinsic motivation. "You're trying to get students to be intrinsically motivated, right?" they ask. The answer is, "partially." The educators in my workshops are recognizing that SDT no longer resembles the goody promising of behaviorism, which is clearly extrinsic. But SDT does not rely only on intrinsic motivation, either. The principles of SDT still draw on extrinsic motivators, but not merely the rewards and punishments typically found inside the classroom. There are many forms of extrinsic motivation, which are diagrammed in figure 1.1.

Student motivation is more broad and varied than the intrinsic/extrinsic division suggests. This is because there are at least four distinct types of extrinsic motivation. Two of these are controlling and therefore undermine students' basic psychological needs. But two of them are autonomy supportive. That is to say, extrinsic motivation is not all bad. You and I, for example, often develop new personal interests that began as extrinsic motivators. I started jogging to please my doctor. But the dozens of marathons and ultramarathons I have completed over the years have been for myself.

In their decades of studying why people do what they do, psychologists Ryan and Deci (2000, 2017) discovered more nuance between extrinsic and intrinsic motivation than had previously been given. Specifically, they noticed how extrinsic motivation is not uniform. Compare, for example, the following extrinsic motivations a student has for attending class (and the corresponding motivational regulation):

- They attend to collect their five participation points. (*External regulation*)
- They attend because that's what good college students are supposed to do. (*Introjected regulation*)
- They attend because they feel that class participation is generally worthwhile. (*Identified regulation*)
- They attend because they feel doing so will allow them to strengthen their career preparation and personal development. (*Integrated regulation*)

In the last two examples, classroom attendance begins as an extrinsic motivator, but the student is beginning to adopt their own reasons for doing so. This means that their behaviors are neither intrinsically motivated nor extrinsically motivated—at least not in the simplistic, "I'm doing this for that," sort of way. This is the process of internalization.

Ryan and Deci have teased apart four different types of extrinsic motivation, which stretch between amotivation (no motivation) and intrinsic motivation.

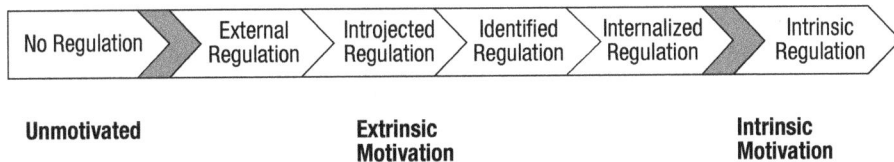

| No Regulation | External Regulation | Introjected Regulation | Identified Regulation | Internalized Regulation | Intrinsic Regulation |

Unmotivated   **Extrinsic Motivation**   **Intrinsic Motivation**

Figure 1.1. Continuum of motivational regulation *Note*. **Ryan and Deci (2000) report that this continuum does not have to be traveled in a stepwise progression. Therefore the arrows are partially misleading. A student might skip, for example, from external regulation to integrated regulation. The right-facing arrows occur in an autonomy-supportive environment. In a controlling environment, the arrows would face to the left.**

When teachers are introduced to the difference between intrinsic and extrinsic motivation, it is clear that intrinsic motivation is the winner. It is preferable to have a student who brings with them to their writing class a deep desire to become a better writer. No amount of promises or threats could dissuade or injure the passion of such a student. This is better than, say, a student who is only after an A or a letter of recommendation from their professor. But there are many forms of extrinsic motivation. Some forms are more satisfying to students than others. The goal of AST is to support the inner regulation and self-determination of students.

CONTINUUM OF EXTRINSIC MOTIVATION

Extrinsic motivation is easily differentiated from amotivation, which is a complete lack of desire, will, and initiative. Extrinsic motivation is also easily differentiated from intrinsic motivation, which grows out of the learner and cannot be influenced by a teacher or college professor. Intrinsic motivation finds its origins in the learner.

There are many forms of extrinsic motivation, however, and they form a continuum between the stupor of amotivation and the magic of intrinsic motivation. The type of extrinsic motivation that borders amotivation in figure 1.1 is just about as weak as amotivation, and the type of extrinsic motivation that borders intrinsic motivation approaches the strength of intrinsic motivation. The relative strength of these motivations is shown in figure 1.2.

As a student moves from left to right along the x-axis of figure 1.2, or along the series of arrows in figure 1.1, the regulation of learning behavior becomes increasingly internalized. On the far left, there is no behavioral self-regulation. A student is unengaged, passive, indifferent, and apathetic. On the far right, where we find intrinsic self-regulation, a student's behaviors, beliefs, and values are completely self-determined.

The workshops in chapters 6 and 7 specify how to support student intrinsic regulation and internalized regulation, respectively.

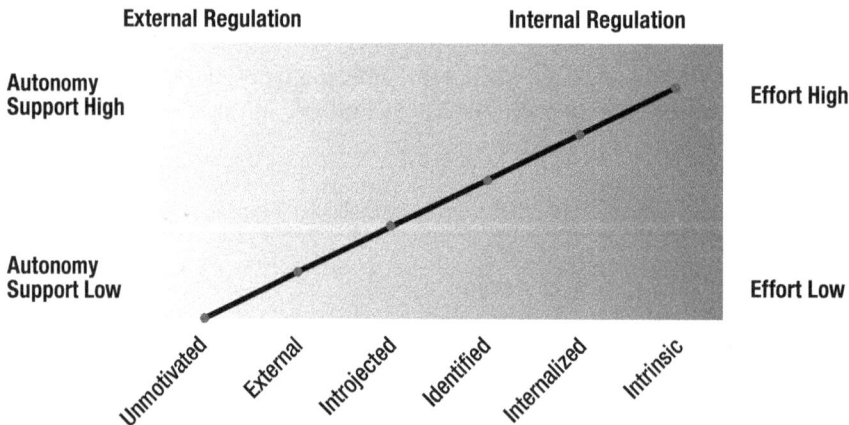

Figure 1.2. Effort and autonomy support of students along the motivation continuum *Note.* **The values in figure 1.2 do not represent real values or real magnitudes. They do, however, illustrate the relative impact of autonomy support on student motivational regulation, and motivational regulation effort, enjoyment, and psychological well-being.**

Internalization and the Regulation of Beliefs, Values, and Behaviors

Another way of talking about motivation is to describe where a person's thoughts and actions are being regulated from. When a student does what they are told, for example, then we can say that their behavioral regulation is external—it finds its origin in the instructor's commands or expectations. When the student decides for themselves what they would like to do, then their behavioral regulation is intrinsic—it finds its origin within the student. But there are many interim steps between external and intrinsic forms of behavioral regulation. When a student listens to and decides to follow a suggestion, then their behavioral regulation is in part external and in part internal. This process of adopting external direction as one's own is called internalization.

NO REGULATION OF BELIEFS, VALUES, AND BEHAVIORS

There is only one type of nonregulation of behaviors, beliefs, and values. These are the unmotivated students who show no interest in the organized learning that their professor has prepared. A student with this kind of regulation is recognizable by their absence, sleeping in class, staring at their phone, ignoring what is happening around them, persistent looks of boredom, or their general expression of apathy. This was the regulation of my students I described in the introduction.

Unmotivated students are difficult to work with, because they are not present to interact with the instructor. It is difficult to support the autonomy of a student who is missing. Of course any one of these behaviors, by itself, does not indicate that a given student (or professor) is unmotivated to learn. Motivation may just be low for learning on a particular day.

It is also important to remember that apathy is a consequence of learning environments that stifle and thwart students' basic psychological needs. By the time students reach college, they have already learned that organized schooling supports or thwarts their autonomy, competence, and relatedness. In my experience, students have learned that school is a place for controlling teachers to make demands. If, however, these same students confront a learning environment that supports their needs, then they will become more self-directed.

In an example biology class, an unmotivated student stays home or sits in the back of class and streams Netflix on their smartphone.

EXTERNAL REGULATION OF BELIEFS, VALUES, AND BEHAVIORS

In SDT, the aim of external regulation "is to strengthen desired, adaptive behaviors through external reinforcement contingencies so the behaviors will be elicited by the reinforcement contingencies to which they have been linked" (Ryan & Deci, 2017, p. 425). This is the model of motivation provided by behaviorism. College faculty are familiar with external regulation: grades, grade point averages, scholarships, awards, grants, certificates, degrees, bonuses, credits, extra credit, and on and on.

External regulation can also occur through praise and selective affirmation. An instructor might be annoyed by students who are quiet during class, yet kind and encouraging to students who participate in discussion. These emotional responses provide the same kind of punishment and rewards that grades provide.

There are two types of external regulation.

Externalized Regulation

Externalized regulation is typified by control. In higher education, this is the kind of unconscionably strict classroom that is caricatured on any film or television show. It is very clear in these classrooms that the instructor is in control of course materials, learning objectives, discussion topics, and student behavior. Anybody who refuses to follow along will be punished. Students are either threatened with severe sanctions for misbehavior, or they are promised As and Bs for doing as they're told.

Students who attend class and study for exams though external regulation are as interested in learning as the previous group (no regulation). The difference is that externally regulated students find in the carrot or stick sufficient motivation to do as they're told. That is to say, they are not as interested in learning as they are interested in whatever learning gets them (such as a college degree).

External regulation seems powerful because it reliably produces the desired performances from students who wouldn't otherwise be interested in performing. As we have seen, however, the quality of student work suffers. Shortcuts are taken. Learning is superficial and quickly forgotten. Steps are followed mindlessly and thoughtlessly. Creativity is low. And so on. Students also suffer blows to their psychological well-being as measured by self-report inventories. A more detailed discussion can be found in Ryan and Deci (2017, chs. 6–7).

In an example biology class, a college student with externalized behavioral regulation wants to know if what Dr. So and So has just said will be on the test. That is to say, the student wants to know if they should bother writing it down or thinking about it at all.

Introjected Regulation

Introjected regulation provides another form of control—specifically psychological control. It is sometimes difficult to recognize introjected regulation when it occurs, because the reasons behind student behavior are not always visible.

Introjection is a psychoanalytic term that describes a belief or value, usually taken from mom or dad (or teacher), that has been accepted completely but without understanding. The belief has been swallowed whole, and it is left undigested. If a belief is undigested, then it cannot be broken down into smaller bits, and these bits cannot be assimilated and integrated into the personality. Introjected beliefs remain intact, and the student who holds the introjected belief remains unchanged. Introjected beliefs are often spoken as rules to live by.

Common introjected beliefs in college students include

- I have to be responsible,
- I need to focus on my studies,

- I shouldn't procrastinate,
- I have to make something of myself,
- I shouldn't miss class,
- the best students make As,
- I need to make sure my professor knows my name,
- the best students talk a lot in class,
- I shouldn't share unless I know that I am right,
- I had better do the reading, and
- I have to learn my professor's biases and then parrot those back on the exam.

A student's introjected regulation to learn comes from a source outside of themselves (e.g., a parent, former teacher, coach, or current instructor). In its introjected form, a student's sentiment that "I had better do the reading" stems from a worry of what might happen were the student's parent to find out that the student partied instead of completing their homework. The student is concerned with whether or not the rule enforcer (i.e., the person who is really in control) will find out.

Instructors play a role in whether a behavior, belief, or value is likely to become introjected by their students. The instructor accomplishes this by implying psychological and social rewards for obedience.

Imagine, for example, that on the first day of class a literature instructor explains how much they love it when their students read poetry on their own for fun. The instructor even smiles thoughtfully as they tell a story of a memorable student who read aloud a scandalous poem by Charles Bukowski, even though this student hadn't been asked to do so and wouldn't receive any sort of academic reward as compensation. In doing so, the instructor has set the bar of achievement for all students who wish to garner their instructor's praise. We might expect that, within a week, hopeful (and slightly bewildered) students will begin arriving to class with library copies of Bukowski and Ginsberg and Burroughs. In this hypothetical example, the students have introjected the belief, "Good students go out of their way to read American Beat Poetry for their own personal edification."

Introjected regulation seems to come from within the student, but it actually comes from teacher (or parent). If we can call external rewards behaviorally manipulating, then introjected motivation is emotionally or psychologically manipulating. External rewards manipulate students with "do this and you'll get that." Emotional manipulation uses phrases such as, "If you don't want to be a huge disappointment to your mom, then you'll get straight As this semester."

Control through introjected regulation can be tricky to identify, even for an instructor who values free thinking and liberal education. For example, listen to this self-reflection from an American historian of education:

> I always welcomed the widest discussion, but, I now know, I still wanted and expected my students to know the text and the lecture material set out for them. Even worse, I now know that although I welcomed discussions, I wanted, above all things, that, after all was said and done, the final conclusions of the class to come out according to my way of thinking. Hence none of the discussions were real discussions, in the sense that it was open and free and inquiring; none of the questions were real questions, in the

sense that they sought to evoke thinking; all of them were loaded, in the sense that I had pretty definite convictions about what I thought were good answers and at times right answers. Hence, I came to the class with subject matter and my students were really instruments by which situations were manipulated to produce the inclusion of what I regarded as desirable subject matter. (Tenenbaum, 1961, p. 311)

The author of this reflection was none other than Samuel Tenenbaum, biographer of the progressive educator William Heard-Kilpatrick. Despite his knowledge that controlled learning is not as productive or need satisfying as internally regulated learning, Tenenbaum realized that he had continued to manipulate his students into thinking his thoughts. The words "my students were really instruments" capture the external regulation that occurs with introjected beliefs, values, and behaviors.

Students who are eager to please their parents and college professors will piously accept without question whatever they are asked to do. Deep down, however, the students are doing so because it is what mom or dad or teacher would have wanted. Because it is manipulating, this form of extrinsic motivation will not be suggested as a goal beyond getting students off of the classroom sidelines.

In an example biology class, a student with introjected motivation works really hard because they need to become a doctor. Not because this is what fascinates the student, but because the student's mother only ever seemed interested when discussing a future career in medicine.

INTERNALIZED REGULATION OF BELIEFS, VALUES, AND BEHAVIORS

Internalization represents one of the root theories of SDT. Internalization is "the process of taking in values, beliefs, or behavioral regulations from external sources and transforming them into one's own" (Ryan & Deci, 2017, p. 180). As you might expect, internalization is crucial to organized classroom learning. Colleges, universities, graduate programs, and professional schools are designed and accredited based on their ability to facilitate the achievement of specifiable learning objectives. With internalization, students take these objectives on as their own objectives, and not as mere hurdles to navigate in exchange for a diploma or degree.

Internalization begins with beliefs, values, and behaviors that are introduced from outside of the student, and they are therefore still considered extrinsic motivators. The difference with internalized regulation is that students begin to adopt these as their own. There are two forms of internalized regulation.

Identified Regulation

Here we see a significant shift from external control to student self-direction. "In acting out of identified regulation," Ryan and Deci (2017) explain, "people are not simply complying with an external or introjected demand but are instead acting out of a belief in the personal importance or perceived value of the activity" (p. 188).

A student who is after an A in botany (external regulation) will be less patient when making mistakes than a student who is starting to believe biology will be beneficial to their future career as a healthcare provider, scientist, or preservationist.

Think of identified motivation as trying on a new outfit. The outfit was chosen by somebody else, but parts of it seem okay. You take the outfit to the fitting room and see how it looks. You recognize parts of it that fit together with your existing wardrobe, but you are not yet ready to build your entire wardrobe around the outfit.

In an example biology class, a student with identified regulation is discovering what it is like to see the world through the eyes of a biologist. Skin is no longer skin but a complex living organ. It is a tedious way of looking at things, and it requires a new vocabulary, but the student believes that acquiring the new vocabulary will likely be beneficial in their career or in the development of a new perspective.

Integrated Regulation

Integrated regulation represents the most personally transformative kind of extrinsic motivation. It is also the most internalized form of regulation short of purely intrinsic regulation. Ryan and Deci (2017) describe it as follows:

> Integrated regulation entails that one bring a value or regulation into congruence with the other aspects of one's self—with one's basic psychological needs and with one's other identifications. [. . .] When achieved, one can experience a more wholehearted endorsement of the behavior or value and an absence of conflict with other abiding identifications. (p. 188)

In psychology courses, students are often confronted with evidence that challenges their cultural beliefs and personal values. For example, "mounting evidence shows that corporal punishment, often referred to as 'spanking,' 'popping,' or 'smacking,' is detrimental to children" (Criss et al., 2021). Yet my students in the American Southeast often hem and haw whenever we discuss whether spanking is beneficial to child development. The presentation of evidence from randomized control trials—that is, the chief method for testing a psychological claim—is often too weak to change long-held personal beliefs about what does or what does not work. In this example, students are resistant; it is too difficult to amend their beliefs and values in order to accommodate new information.

Now imagine a student who reviews the evidence and begins to think differently about how they will raise their own children. This is an example of integrated regulation. In it we see that the student has not merely acquired a new belief or value; they have amended their existing beliefs and values—restructuring who they are in the process.

In a course on social problems, for example, a student whose regulation is integrated will become an ambassador for social justice and change. By wholeheartedly adopting the social justice perspective, existing values will be corrected or amended in order that they all fit together. Therefore this student does not only look at the world through new eyes, but participates in it through a new worldview.

In an example biology class, a student has begun applying biological principles to their daily lives. They start to interpret their relationships as would a biologist—

using words like symbiosis and parasite. They start looking more carefully at nutrition labels, and will probably begin to rely less and less on hearsay—choosing instead to investigate data for themselves.

INTRINSIC REGULATION OF BELIEFS, VALUES, AND BEHAVIORS

With intrinsic motivation, a student no longer needs a diploma or degree to continue learning. This happens daily, of course, but it has fallen out of fashion to describe daily and personal learnings as true scholarly learning. This is unfortunate, because the words "scholarly" and "school" are derived from the Greek word for leisure, which is σχολα or *scholá*.

Looking at the motivational continuum, the graph, and all of the descriptions that follow them, it is easy to imagine how teacher and student morale would improve the further right on the continuum that learning occurs. This is precisely the objective of AST. It is little surprise that AST has produced the kinds of outcomes that were described in chapter 1.

The seven strategies that will be introduced in chapter 2 have been demonstrated to reliably elicit intrinsic and internalized regulation in students.

Autonomy-Supportive Teaching

Now it is time to look back to the three vignettes that opened this book. Using what you've learned about SDT, take another gander at the various instructor responses.

Vignette 1, Where Online Students Missed the First Deadline

In vignette 1, in which 40% of students have missed the first deadline in an online course, an instructor will be justifiably concerned. At first, I suspect that any of the four options might seem helpful in remedying the situation. Only one option, however, will reliably succeed in reversing the problem. The other three options will only make things worse.

Option 1, which was giving students a one-time extension, but reminding them that you cannot keep moving deadlines, is an example of providing course structure in a controlling way. Structure—even though it might seem restricting and limiting, and might therefore inhibit student self-direction—is helpful if it is provided in an autonomy-supportive way. This is particularly true in online courses, which will be described in more detail in chapters 3 and 10. When offered in an autonomy-supportive way, course structure helps students understand what is expected of them so they can plan accordingly. Students are not likely to be surprised or confused in courses that provide lots of structure, and will therefore feel more comfortable exercising their autonomy. In option 1, however, the course structure is reinforced in a way that reminds students that the instructor is in control, and that the students must do as they're told. (You might try to think of a way of providing structure that is not controlling.)

In option 2, which was telling students to complete the assignment whenever they feel like it, the instructor abandons the course structure that was already in place. At the beginning of the semester, students were given deadlines. Now those deadlines have been repealed. Students will be wondering what else is going to change. Rather than adjust an expectation or make an informed change to the course, this instructor has effectively told their students, "Anything goes." This has been called a laissez-faire teaching style (Aelterman et al., 2019), and it thwarts student autonomy. The lack of clear expectations, resources, instruction, and requirements forces students to become withdrawn. It is very important to realize that withdrawal does not represent student baseline motivation. College students, just like humans in general, are inherently motivated by self-direction, as we saw in chapter 1. But laissez-faire classrooms make this self-direction difficult or impossible. Therefore, option 2 thwarts student autonomy.

Option 3 is an example of an autonomy-supportive teaching strategy. In particular, it is an example of "Taking Students' Perspective." We know that students in online courses tend to juggle more nonacademic responsibilities than do their peers in traditional face-to-face courses. Students choose online courses for reasons of scheduling flexibility and time convenience (Harris & Martin, 2012). But online students are not lazy. In my experience, students in online courses show unbelievable levels of determination. I have had students working multiple jobs and taking care of relatives and children, all while maintaining a full course load. In vignette 1, the missed deadline might actually say nothing at all about student interest or engagement. The problem might be something simple and fixable. It might be a problem of poor course design, poor online infrastructure, poor communication, or something else the instructor has not anticipated. By asking the students directly, this problem can be discovered and corrected. For example, I once learned that students were expecting an emailed notification for upcoming deadlines, which I had not programmed. I got in touch with our online specialist and learned how to automate these emails, and never had that problem again.

Finally, option 4 looks and sounds like a best teaching practice, but it is an example of a controlling teaching style—specifically a psychologically controlling teaching style. Controlling teachers manipulate students into performing the desired learning behaviors. An instructor might use grades or the threat of punishment to entice students to follow course instructions. In this situation, the instructor is the one holding the strings that get students to move about. When humans have externally regulated motivation, they feel as if they are pawns being moved about in somebody else's game. And who wants to feel like that? (The research suggests that nobody wants to feel that way.)

Controlling teaching, and the external behavioral regulation it leads to, is the opposite of autonomy support. In the end, in particular the controlling teaching (option 4) and chaotic teaching (option 2) will eventually lead to the situation described in vignette 3: student boredom and apathy. This is important, because it means that student apathy and boredom are a consequence of learning environments. The students do wish to learn, but they have not been supported in their learning.

Vignette 2, The One with Lethargic Graduate Students

In vignette 2, you observe that your graduate students are sleepy during a class period in which a difficult concept is being introduced. How might you support students' need for autonomy, competence, and relatedness?

Certainly not by following option 1, which is reminding them that they can leave as soon as that day's objective has been completed. This is a "do this, get that" sort of exchange. Students are told that if they follow the instructor's wishes, then they can get what they probably want the most, which is to leave. The behavioral regulation is external, because the instructor has selected the target behavior. But the reward has also been selected by the instructor. In this option, the instructor assumes that the students have no interest in the course—that they couldn't possibly be self-directed learners. Students would likely experience stifled competence and autonomy.

With option 2, you observe your students' lethargy and ask for suggestions on how to approach the difficult objective. This is a combination of two autonomy supportive strategies: "Acknowledging Negative Feelings" and "Taking Students' Perspective." By observing students' low energy, you are acknowledging that they are not eager to kick the doors down on today's lesson. If this is observed without judgment, and without any hint that your students ought to feel guilty or irresponsible, then they will feel more comfortable and capable as learners—that they can accomplish difficult objectives even when they are not feeling 100%. By asking for student suggestions on how to proceed, the students themselves get to participate in the direction of the class. Furthermore, the students will benefit from the input of one another.

Option 3—ending class immediately—is a chaotic response. Even though they are not thrilled to come to class, the students have gone through the trouble of getting there. Canceling a scheduled class just as it is beginning disrupts the course structure that students have come to expect, and it punishes energy levels that are anything short of effervescent. Like option 1, ending class right away assumes that students have no self-directed interest in learning.

Option 4, which is following the course schedule as planned, and pointing out how today's class period fits in with the overall course objectives, is another example of providing structure. This time, however, the structure is offered in an autonomy supportive way—specifically "Giving Explanatory Rationale." The explanation about the importance of today's course helps students better internalize the objectives for the day. This is because they are given all of the information that the instructor has about the class period, and they are free to draw their own conclusions.

After reviewing the possible responses to vignettes 1 and 2, I hope it is clear that student motivation in vignette 3 is a consequence of learning experiences that have stifled students' psychological needs. AST will reverse this process, leading to increases in student self-directed interest, engagement, curiosity, and so on.

Autonomy-Supportive Teaching

Teachers are autonomy-supportive when they actively create classroom conditions to support students' basic psychological needs and strengthen students' inner motivational resources. Supporting student autonomy requires a shift in teacher emphasis from curricular content by itself to curricular content within the context of a particular group of students. AST recognizes and accepts that optimal learning begins with student motivation, and it creates conditions to facilitate this process.

Any kind of classroom, learning outcome, or discipline can benefit from AST. Piles of examples demonstrating its usefulness can be found in elementary, secondary, postsecondary, graduate, and professional schools, to say nothing of organizational management. In chapter 3, I look specifically at the research that has been done in higher education over the past few years. But right now I want to quickly point at the prodigious volume of impressive findings about the benefits of AST in general over the past few decades.

When learning in an autonomy-supported way, students' classroom habits and activities continue well after their courses have ended. They demonstrate higher proficiencies in skill development, participate more, and feel more confident in their personal abilities related to their classes. In a review article written over ten years ago, Reeve (2009) provides a table organizing the research supporting AST along with the more than 50 references to studies in which these outcomes were tested.

A database of free articles can be found by searching online at www.selfdetermi nationtheory.org.

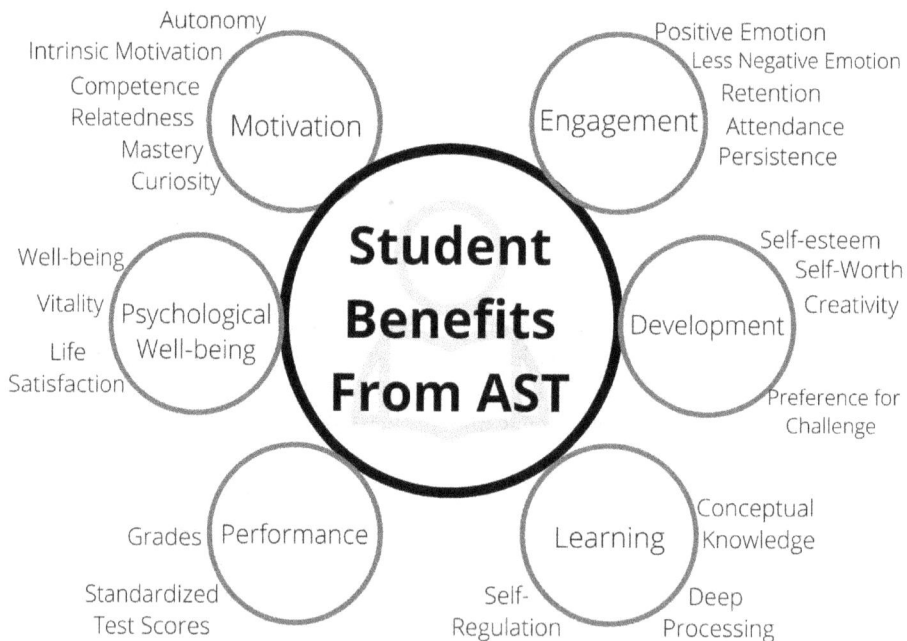

Figure 2.1.   Student outcomes with instructor-provided autonomy support

Seven Strategies for Supporting Student Autonomy

Throughout this book, the primary focus is on supporting student autonomy in college courses, and this includes the seven strategies that will be described shortly. A second book could easily be written about strategies for providing course structure—syllabi, activity design, lecturing, and so on. Methods for providing structure will appear throughout the book, but this is not a main focus.

Education researcher Johnmarshall Reeve has made it his professional mission to develop instructional resources and training programs to promote and support AST at all levels of education. The following seven steps have been consolidated from the many articles of his on the subject specifically (Reeve, 2016; Reeve & Cheon, 2021).

STRATEGY 1: AUTONOMY-SUPPORTIVE TEACHERS ADOPT THEIR STUDENTS' PERSPECTIVE

The first strategy for supporting student autonomy begins at the course planning stage with the questions, "Where are my students coming from?" "What do my students already know?" "Where are my students hoping to go?" "What do my students enjoy?" and so on. This is not pandering to student interests; it is building on the strengths, insights, and interests that students bring with them. In a general psychology course, for example, I get about one week to spend on a 1,000-page document (*DSM-5*) and the many thousands of pages of criticisms it has received. Because I have asked them directly, however, I know that my students are particularly interested in attention deficit disorder, autism, and schizophrenia. I do not have time to go into the hundreds of psychiatric disorders, so I choose those with which students have some familiarity and interest. They get to start the section of psychopathology thinking "Oh! I know what that is! My cousin got that!"

The same goes for activities, assessments, and feedback until I have thought about every aspect of the course from the students' perspective. Teachers who think to themselves, "that activity didn't go very well," and who then try something different the next time around are already doing this. But they would have better luck if they let students be a part of the redesign process.

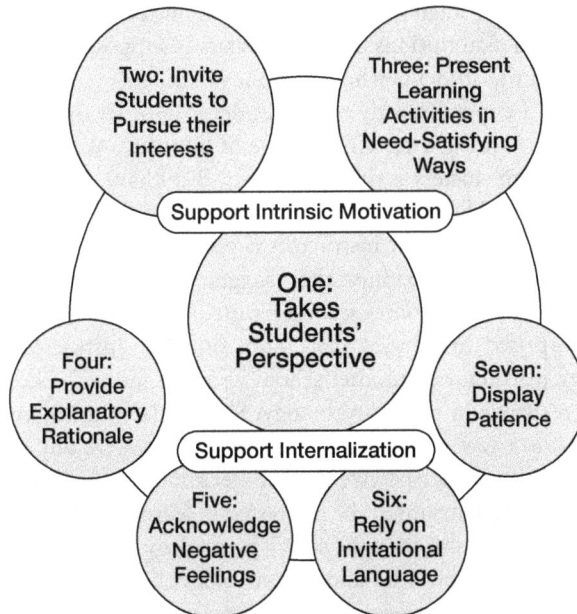

Figure 2.2. The seven autonomy-supportive teaching strategies. *Note:* Earlier lists (Reeve, 2016) included only six AST strategies, and strategies two and three were combined. Adapted from Reeve and Cheon, 2021, p. 56.

My Experience Taking Students' Perspective

Taking the perspective of my college students is a strange practice. When seated at my desk and chewing on the end of a pen, I can only ever think about the class from my point of view, imagining it as though I am 20 years younger. I suspect that, with three college degrees and a passion for writing, I make a poor representative for my students, who are mostly young black women from Atlanta, USA, and who are the first of their families to go to college.

I do my best. I pick topics and resources that I, a middle-aged and middle-class white guy from Michigan, USA, imagine that my students will find most interesting. I organize these resources around activities that I, a middle-aged . . . (etc.) imagine young black women . . . (etc.) will find most interesting. By the time I have planned a week of courses, the activities and topics and resources are still many times removed from my students' points of view.

I plan a class period around what I think my students will find interesting and important and meaningful, but I also explain to my students how clueless I probably am. The session goes well or poorly depending on how good I was at anticipating their interests. But my efforts to take their perspective have only just begun.

Next, I hand out pieces of scrap paper the size of a notecard and ask my students for their honest feedback. I ask them, "What did you like about class?" "What do you want to do more of?" "What was missing?" and "If you could design it yourself, then what would you do?"

Then I read the anonymous feedback. I learn, for example, that I didn't give them enough time working in small groups, and that the concept of "authoritative parenting" was unclear. In a journal, I record methods for integrating their suggestions into the next class.

I also reflect on my personal concerns. For example, "I'm worried that students will get bored working in small groups, so I rush us on to the next thing." This helps me recognize my own assumptions about how class is supposed to go, and it leads to me checking in with the students who I imagine are bored.

In other words, I depend mostly on my students in order to understand students' points of view. This requires a certain measure of humility, at least at first. I feel like I'm admitting that I am clueless as their instructor. But I have come to learn that this is not how students see it. They are more gracious than I could have imagined. They are surprised to find that one of their instructors is genuinely interested in their perspective, which they have realized because their suggestions are being implemented. The more I do this, the more it becomes second nature.

I am now surprised by courses that adopt only the instructor's perspective. A young psychology instructor at another school wrote to me and asked for my recommendation for a textbook in social psychology. She had been using my (2016) general psychology book for a few years, and wondered if there were any social psychology books that offered a similar perspective. I asked her about her goals for the course, and what she thought her students might be interested in learning. She went on to describe her dissertation, and how she thought social psychology ought to be treated. It was clear that this instructor knew a lot about psychology, but I wondered if she had her finger on her own pulse, or on the pulse of her students. Together we created a list of possible topics with which students could easily engage—topics that included recent events in their region, political issues, social media, online learning, and so on. I will admit that I got excited thinking about such a course!

STRATEGY 2: AUTONOMY-SUPPORTIVE TEACHERS INVITE STUDENTS TO PURSUE THEIR INTERESTS

Strategies 2 and 3 are geared toward supporting student intrinsic motivation. This is where the regulation of beliefs, behaviors, and values finds its origin within the students. In order to connect learning objectives to intrinsic motivation, students must be encouraged to identify where those connections occur.

Math faculty invite students to pursue their interests when they ask about real personal problems that students face—such as calculating rate of return on an investment or interest accrued on a loan—that can be solved using mathematics. Writing faculty do this when they invite students to choose the style and format of the writing that they do for class—styles that they use in their everyday lives, such as writing social media posts, text messages, journal entries, and so on.

Student interests can also be solicited for course topics. Students can be asked what appeals to them about the course in question, and the list of topics can be used to build a course schedule.

In each of these examples, students are not cut free to do as they wish. They are included in the course development process so that the course design represents their unique interests. Then the instructor uses these topics to design activities, and works with students to achieve course outcomes.

While it might seem implausible to practice this strategy with a lecture hall of 500 students, it is not impossible. I regularly use learning management software to create surveys with about 50 possible course topics, and ask students to rate them in terms of their level of interest. I design the course around the topics that receive the most votes.

My Experience Inviting Students to Pursue Their Interests

I have begun the practice of handing the equivalent of blank syllabi to my students on the first day of class. I tell them that I have to submit completed syllabi to the main office by the end of the first week, and that I need their help to make that happen. I give them a series of questions to consider, such as what sorts of skills they would like to develop and which topics they find most interesting. (If the course in question has a required learning objective, then I ask students for their insight about how we might best achieve that objective.)

By listening to and observing student affect, I feel out whether we will do an impromptu discussion and vote, a question-and-answer period, or if we need more time to think about it independently and return to vote on it later.

In a course I am teaching right now—an introductory psychology course—the question about student interests unleashed a tidal wave of questions, insights, personal stories, and general discussion. And this was 10 minutes into the first day of class, where students are generally trying to feel out the learning environment in which they've found themselves. At one point, 90% of students had their hands in the air, waiting for their turn to share what they would like to have included in the course.

STRATEGY 3: AUTONOMY-SUPPORTIVE TEACHERS PRESENT LEARNING ACTIVITIES IN NEED-SATISFYING WAYS

As I described in chapter 1, humans have three basic psychological needs, which are for autonomy, competence, and relatedness. The satisfaction of these needs leads to greater psychological well-being.

In order to present learning activities in need-satisfying ways, the instructor must do their best to support student autonomy, competence, and relatedness.

Autonomy

Student autonomy is supported by following the strategies in this book. For example, students can be given choices, they can participate in course design or selection of learning resources, or they can collaborate on the assessment process.

Competence

Student competence is supported when instructors make sure that course activities are not too difficult (and therefore demoralizing to students) or too easy (and therefore boring to students). By regularly checking in with students or performing mini assessments, instructors can get a feel for the optimal level of challenge.

Relatedness

Student relatedness is supported when they are invited to interact or work together with each other.

My Experience Presenting Learning Activities in Need-Satisfying Ways

As the autonomy-supportive teaching workshop began to pick up, participating faculty started wondering what it might look like in their classrooms once they got the hang of supporting student autonomy. One participant in particular asked if she could visit my classroom. I told her that she could, but that I wasn't going to guarantee anything exceptional.

She came by during a class period that seemed, to me, to have low interest and low engagement. But my colleague was amazed. "Are they always like that?" she asked.

I admitted that they were sometimes more energetic, and I acknowledged my role in the lower-than-usual enthusiasm. My colleague explained how impressed she was with how confident the students were while leading the class discussion, and asked how that came about.

I explained that I wasn't sure.

What stood out to me was how the energy level didn't seem that high. Upon reflection, however, every student who was present had participated in the discussion. Students agreed and disagreed with one another, and they asked thoughtful questions. In other words, the discussion was a group effort. This meant that it required that each student take a measure of ownership in the class.

How did this happen?

For over a decade, I have been trying to facilitate meaningful classroom discussions. As recently as two years ago my efforts typically resulted in vanishingly small numbers of students in attendance while I lectured at the lectern. But on the day my colleague visited, I said almost nothing. Students did most of the work.

The scenario is not shocking once I considered how inner motivational resources are recruited. Self-determination theory lists three main motivators: autonomy, competence, and relatedness. Most faculty are happy if their students are self-directed, challenging themselves, and interacting with each other. It turns out that students are happiest when they are doing so, too.

STRATEGY 4: AUTONOMY-SUPPORTIVE TEACHERS PROVIDE EXPLANATORY RATIONALE

Strategies 4 through 7 help students internalize beliefs, values, and behaviors. These strategies are useful when the learning objectives are something other than what students might choose to do in their free time. The first of these is providing explanatory rationale.

When providing explanatory rationale, the instructor makes clear the purpose of any learning activity. By doing so, students no longer have to ask the question, "Why is this important?"

As college instructors, we have spent a lot of time selecting the best learning resources, the most beneficial activities, and the most helpful assessments. We have experienced firsthand what seems to work well and what works poorly. The evidence shows us that it is helpful to students when we share with them our insights about why and how we have organized our courses. If lots of repetition is helpful for nailing down a skill, then let your students know.

I remember a logic course I took while in college. I found all of the logical syllogisms so boring, and the series of proofs we had to solve were mind numbing. But this professor would walk around the classroom pumping his scrawny arms like he was lifting weights, and he would repeat, "You've got to exercise your logic muscles." I stopped feeling like I was doing busywork, and started feeling like I was in the weight room conditioning my mind.

When I do demonstrations of psychological phenomena (such as with perceptual illusions), my students don't need any explanation because those activities are more exciting than listening to me talk. When I give a lecture on the Gestalt principles of perception, however, their eyes glaze over. If, instead, I began that lecture with "have you ever come across a website that was impossible to navigate—like, you couldn't figure out what to click and how to get around?" before talking about how Gestalt theory provides the why, then I would be giving my students an explanatory rationale. Notice how different "Gestalt theory" sounds when it is introduced as something you have experienced.

My Experience Providing Explanatory Rationale

When I design courses before a semester begins, I think through all of the objectives, activities, and resources I will use. I feel like I am planning an elaborate meal with multiple courses and wine pairings. I have reasons for everything. The research tells me that it is helpful to students when I am transparent about what I am doing. There are no secret recipes in an autonomy-supportive classroom.

I was surprised to learn that some of my reasons for course activities were rooted in my own insecurities as a professor. I observed that it was important to me that students be productive. I noticed how I was disappointed whenever we spent the entire class period talking about, for example, how students were afraid to pump gas (petrol) at the gas station after dark. But quietly I would think to myself, "Well, what sort of evidence will we have to show that our time together this morning was well spent?"

During the next class period I would open by saying something such as, "Write a one-page reflection on what we talked about during last class," which they would do diligently after borrowing some paper and staring at the wall for a few minutes. Were I to give them my rationale for the writing assignment, however, I would have been forced to say, "You have to write a page or so because I am worried that my colleagues will think me too lax a professor if all we do during a class period is talk."

I actually shared a version of this with my students one time, and do you know how they responded? Every single one of them agreed to write a paper of any length if I thought it would make me look better for my annual review. They would do so even though they didn't feel like it would be a valuable learning experience for them personally. (I thanked them for their selflessness, but declined to take them up on their offer.)

Following this principle has required that I reevaluate some of my compulsory learning practices. I realized that I had filled the semester with busywork whenever I was unsure of what would be best in helping students achieve the course objectives—such as always assigning homework over extended weekends.

STRATEGY 5: AUTONOMY-SUPPORTIVE TEACHERS ACKNOWLEDGE NEGATIVE FEELINGS

Humans are more than walking and talking intellects. This goes for college professors, too, even though we have earned advanced degrees using intellectualization. We still spend the majority of our lives feeling—happy, sad, angry, upset, excited, nervous, worried, uncertain, and so on.

AST scholars have shown that acknowledging this emotional world in students helps those students become more tolerant of and open to learning activities. Feelings of anger or frustration, no matter where they are coming from, result in defensiveness. This defensiveness, if it is not acknowledged and understood, will interrupt the ordinary flow and exchange of information such as a description of the classroom activity. Without realizing it, a defensive student will project the reason for this defensiveness onto their instructor or the activity. When the instructor recognizes the defensiveness in the student, and does so without judgment or wish that the student be or feel any other way, then the student will feel invited to become aware of their own emotional state. They will no longer feel like they have to play defense.

Faculty love to complain. So do students. But nobody likes to hear about how unhelpful their complaining is. They usually don't want a solution, either. They just want to complain. As American community college administrator Matt Reed (2013) has explained, grumpy college faculty are happy faculty. Students are no different.

Students are also like faculty in that they are not unidimensional. Students bring personal problems with them into the classroom. Sometimes these problems disrupt classroom activities, and it is easy to mistake the classroom for the source of the problem. This is where it helps to have a degree in psychology. Thankfully, a psychology degree is not a prerequisite to acknowledging and accepting negative affect of students.

Years ago, I was teaching a research methods course when a student walked in ten minutes late, bringing the temperature down in the classroom noticeably as he did so. He sat brooding in the back while the other students were working in small groups. I called him to the front and asked if maybe his mind was somewhere else, and he explained to me how terrible I was as a professor. I nodded my understanding, and asked if it was possible that maybe something else was going on. We continued the conversation in the hallway once it became clear that the problem was something personal. In the end, I learned that the student was temporarily homeless and sleeping on couches in dormitory common rooms. He was having trouble keeping up appearances. More specifically, he was embarrassed that he hadn't showered in several days.

The point isn't that I solved his tragic problem (I didn't, but he later did). The point is that it is easy to overlook the emotional world of others. William James once described humans as a drop of intellect in an ocean of feeling (in Tenenbaum, 1961). When you acknowledge a student's emotion, you are acknowledging them. You are seeing them. Noticing them.

My Experience Acknowledging Negative Feelings

It came as somewhat of a shock to me when I realized that students do not sit in their dorm rooms waiting for the next time we met together as a class. Of course I knew this on some level, yet I still expected them to be sitting in their seats one minute before the hour eagerly waiting for class to begin.

I'm embarrassed to admit how many years it took me to realize that students have rich and creative lives outside of the classroom, and that when they're not with me they are probably not thinking about me. This means that the irritations and frustrations and anger and sadness that they exhibit in the classroom are probably not directed at me, either.

It is possible to accept that a student is angry without this meaning that the student wishes for all of their problems to be solved. I have applied the same way of thinking to my role as committee chair, too. There is no rule that says everyone has to be on the edge of their seat in order for a university committee to be effective. But how often does it seem okay for a committee member to say, "I think this is a waste of time," without the committee chair to fall out of said chair in an effort to make the committee member happy (or guilting them into a change of attitude)? Can the committee chair listen to and accept the committee member's negative feelings without trying to change them? If they can, then the committee chair will succeed in supporting the autonomy of their committee members.

I am learning to accept that students have other things that they would rather be doing than participating in my class. This doesn't mean that class time will be unproductive or that they will not learn anything valuable. It only means that their priorities are different from my own.

STRATEGY 6: AUTONOMY-SUPPORTIVE TEACHERS USE INVITATIONAL LANGUAGE

When providing autonomy support to their students, teachers do not abandon their favorite lectures, activities, or assessments. But these are introduced using informational, nonpressuring language. Autonomy-supportive teachers avoid words such as "shouldn't," "can't," "must," and "ought to," along with the raised eyebrows, finger wagging, or head shaking that so often accompany these words. Instead of, "You have to read Skinner's *Walden II* before next Monday," autonomy-supportive teachers might say, "Psychologists were not only interested in laboratory experiments. Some designed utopic communes using state of the art psychological principles, such as Fred Skinner. I don't think it works. Do you? Read *Walden II* if you want to discuss it with me on Monday."

Using nonpressuring language does not mean being wishy washy, such as with the statement, "You can do it or not; I don't care." But it does generally mean being open to the possibility that there is another way to accomplish a particular objective. "I thought that it would be best if students worked on these word problems in small groups. How does that sound?" Of course, the instructor in this example would have to be willing to make a change if the students felt that it might be necessary to do so.

My Experience Using Invitational Language

I think that most college instructors use invitational language when introducing a new topic or activity. It is only really in satire that a professor makes demands on students with little more justification than "because I said so."

The way that invitational language makes its appearance in my classroom is a tentative formulation of classroom activities and materials. I like to invite students to participate in course design, as I have explained earlier, which includes identifying learning objectives, requirements, attendance policy, and so forth. But students aren't always willing participants. I might say something such as, "I have learned that students prefer to have a stated attendance policy, even though I don't personally care for one. I thought that we might discuss possible attendance policies as a class, and then see where we land." This is an open invitation for their participation. Because it is not a mandate or requirement, students will be free not to participate. If I have introduced the activity using my explanatory rationale, and if I am acknowledging students' negative feelings (including their unwillingness to participate), then my students will understand what their participation is for, and that they can participate in any way that they choose.

Students will ask their questions to determine whether or not the invitation is sincere, and then they will either volunteer suggestions or sit quietly. If the latter, then I explain that we can leave the issue for the time being, but will return to it at a later point.

In other words, the objective, which in this case is determining the attendance policy, remains an important activity even though it has not been mandated in a controlling way. Perhaps students are not very courageous on the first day of class. After all, they were probably expecting to be told what to do. It is not easy recruiting independent motivations for classroom work when students have never been given such an opportunity.

I do my best to follow the rhythms of student interest and energy when new activities are introduced or new topics are explored. During a particularly passionate discussion one semester, it became clear that students were eager to exercise more self-direction with the course than they had previously. Upon recognizing this, I invited a volunteer to plan the next classroom discussion, an invitation that was accepted immediately. (And this student did an excellent job.)

STRATEGY 7: AUTONOMY-SUPPORTIVE TEACHERS PRACTICE PATIENCE

Student learning styles and speeds are as varied as student personalities. If it takes longer to complete an activity than you had expected, then it might be necessary to modify the course schedule to accommodate this extra time. Doing so requires patience.

Less obvious, however, is what to do when some students achieve proficiency quickly while others lag behind. How can you be patient with some without boring the others? Challenge is necessary for keeping students engaged, but course learning outcomes represent only a tiny fraction of available challenges for students. Accelerated students could be challenged with teaching, for example, or with creating resources for the class. This recognizes their psychological need for relatedness, and carrying it out requires student self-direction. More examples for troubleshooting these types of problems are provided in chapter 9.

My Experience Practicing Patience

In graduate school, my peers decided that my spirit animal was a hummingbird, because I could maintain a high level of energy and focus for long periods of time (and I lived on a diet of mostly sugar). This has followed me to my career as a college professor. What committee members imagine will take six months to complete, I imagine will take only six days. But students are on a different scale entirely. Consequently, I have had to adjust my perspective in the classroom.

To take into consideration the optimal pace of learning for my students, I try to introduce activities, concepts, and procedures gently and carefully. I am always on the lookout for booby traps—an ambiguous concept or counterintuitive idea that might trip a student up. I probably overdo it with definitions and examples. I would rather my students say, "Yes, I know what you mean," than have them sit politely but vacantly.

If I am introducing one of Erikson's stages of development, such as "autonomy versus shame and doubt," then I will immediately spot "autonomy" and "shame" as possible booby traps. So I will give lots of definitions and examples until my students begin finishing my sentences. "A good synonym for autonomy is *self-direction*. When you get your driver's license and can drive yourself to the movie theater, you are exercising your newfound *autonomy*." And so on. If introduced this way, students seem to be more likely to give their own examples or ask questions.

If, as I'm giving an example, I can feel the student interest level waning—phones come out, heads go down on desks, and so on—then I move on to the next booby trap.

With this approach, students are in control of the pace of class. It is not unusual to fill up an entire hour with student examples of autonomy and shame. These will sometimes get very personal, which is evidence that students are engaged in a deep and meaningful way.

The Gestalt of Autonomy-Supportive Teaching

In the psychology of perception, there is this idea of a perceptual Gestalt ("whole") in which the whole is greater than its component parts. Take a bicycle as an example. A bicycle has wheels, tires, pedals, pedal arms, chainrings, chain, a frame, and so on. But adding these parts together into a pile will never give you transportation. It is only when combined in a particular way that these separate parts disappear into one working bicycle. Moreover, if one of the components breaks down, all of the other components are affected. A wobbling bottom bracket interferes with the pedal stroke, which upsets balance in the handlebars.

The same goes for AST. After practicing the strategies separately for a while, you will begin to realize that it is impossible to give explanatory rationale without taking your students' perspective; and it is impossible to use invitational language without practicing patience or acknowledging negative feelings. They're all connected. If you find that you are having trouble being patient, then you will probably also notice a change across each of the AST strategies. Strengthen one strategy and thereby strengthen the others. Neglect one strategy, and thereby neglect the others.

In summary, AST is triply attractive in that (1) it emphasizes learning outcomes that are personally meaningful and significant, (2) it is supported by hundreds of studies, and (3) it can be introduced into any classroom format and integrated into any teaching style. AST doesn't ask teachers to become anything other than themselves. In the following chapter, I will present the evidence that AST works for college students.

CHAPTER 3

Evidence Supporting Autonomy-Supportive Teaching in Higher Education

In 2020, medical school faculty Adam Neufield and Greg Malin at the University of Saskatchewan, Canada, used a sample of 183 medical students to test the relationship between student-perceived autonomy support and psychological well-being. "The results," Neufield and Malin write, "demonstrate how support or hindrance of medical students' basic psychological needs for motivation can explain (mediate) the relationship between their perceptions of instructor autonomy-support and their PWB [psychological well-being]" (p. 654). That is to say, when students felt that their autonomy, competence, and relatedness were supported by faculty, they experienced greater levels of psychological well-being (as measured by the Psychological Well-being Scale; Ryff & Singer, 2008).

Later that year, a pair of medical students replied to the article in a letter to the editor of the same journal. The students were generally in support of AST, but felt that Neufield and Malin had been more than a little naïve in their recommendation that medical faculty use AST practices. The students write, "[b]eing able to have an input allows us to gain more from the session and we feel we learn the most when teaching is done in this way. However, we acknowledge that instructor autonomy-support is only practical in certain situations" (p. 1430). Et cetera. They go on to explain how instructors couldn't possibly support the autonomy of 400 students in a lecture hall, and a busy doctor likely wouldn't have the time to respond to students individually. "Therefore," the medical students Duguid, Duguid, and Bryan (2020) conclude, "some students are at risk of getting forgotten about" (p. 1430). They recommend that lecture–exam instruction be reserved for certain topics.

It is clear from their letter that these medical students had come to expect a particular style of instruction from their faculty. It isn't that these students felt as though the traditional style of didactic teaching and learning was optimal or even enjoyable ("tedious" is the word they used). They just couldn't imagine medical school any other way. The letter is their way of saying to Drs. Neufield and Malin, "we appreciate your optimism, but, let's be real: it'll never work in med school."

The letter captures my own skepticism when first reading about AST and all that it promised. I thought it unlikely that the SDT folks were teaching six and seven courses per semester, or that those professors weren't teaching at schools with low to middling academic performance and retention. I figured that AST could only work for students who were already highly autonomous—that is, students who didn't really need it.

But it does work—even in those unique cases where Duguid et al. (2020) were certain that it wouldn't. Neufield and Malin (2021) replied in a follow-up letter where they took a moment to address a common misconception about autonomy support. They explain, "[a]utonomy-supportive teaching applies in all teaching contexts, including large groups, lectures, clinical encounters, and problem-based learning" (p. 238). They go on to address the large lecture halls identified by Duguid et al. (2020) as inhospitable to AST:

> To be autonomy-supportive in large group settings or those that might involve less student participation (e.g. a didactic anatomy lecture), the instructor could state, "We recognize this content is heavy for students. To help everyone navigate this, we will schedule breaks, welcome questions or suggestions, incorporate sample cases and discuss the answers, and provide clinical practice." (p. 238)

In a single opening statement, this hypothetical instructor has given "emotional support, provided structured guidance, nurtured students' interests, optimized the level of challenge, and communicated value in the topic" (p. 238). Neufield and Malin reflect themselves on how easy AST is to practice, and close by explaining that it "is more about establishing positive, non-controlling learning environments, and less about group sizes or learning topics" (p. 238).

For those of you teaching in graduate or doctoral programs, Neufield and Malin (2020) provide a list of sample autonomy-supportive practices you might try along with a list of controlling techniques to avoid.

Evidence that AST Works in Higher Education

In what follows, I share a series of recently published studies that demonstrate the breadth of applicability of AST in higher education. I have organized some of these contexts into a diagram in figure 3.1. I feel it is worth mentioning that I was unable to find a higher education context in which AST failed to increase learning objectives or student psychological well-being. The evidence provided in this chapter is not intended to be exhaustive. Instead, I have chosen those contexts, demographics, and disciplines in which I felt (and my reviewers felt) AST might not work. The previous exchange, for example, is what I found when looking for evidence that AST wouldn't work in graduate programs. All studies have taken place in the past eight years.

PHYSICAL EDUCATION AND OTHER GENERAL EDUCATION COURSES

In the United States, college students are often required to take a course in health or physical education. This course usually belongs to a list of required classes called the

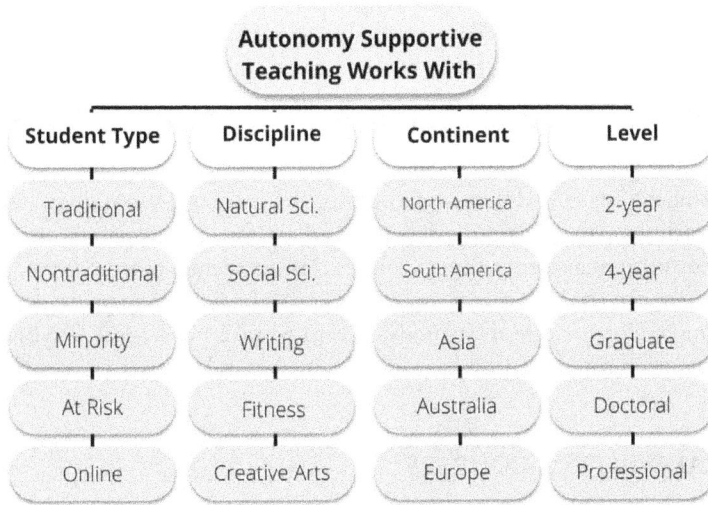

Autonomy Supportive Teaching Works With

Student Type	Discipline	Continent	Level
Traditional	Natural Sci.	North America	2-year
Nontraditional	Social Sci.	South America	4-year
Minority	Writing	Asia	Graduate
At Risk	Fitness	Australia	Doctoral
Online	Creative Arts	Europe	Professional

Figure 3.1.   Breadth of applicability of AST in higher education

general education core. General education courses provide breadth across the arts, humanities, and sciences. One of the issues that general education faculty face is that their students find themselves in courses they wouldn't choose on their own—such as a future physical therapist taking a course in art appreciation. It can be discouraging as a professor to have students yawning or complaining about a course in the professor's specialty area, because the course was one the student felt compelled to take.

This discouragement is even stronger when a professor feels like the course is important for more than intellectual edification. This was the case for Alan Beck, a physical education professor who has organized a community project to increase physical activity in rural populations in Missouri, USA. Beck views physical education courses as one of the few opportunities to save students from lifetimes of health problems and decreased quality of life.

The same problem is found in psychology courses that teach students strategies for increasing life satisfaction, sociology courses that teach students about diversity and social justice, economics courses that teach students financial literacy, writing courses that teach students about self-expression and communication, and so on.

Beck and his colleague Aaron Diehr (2017) describe the problem faced by physical education faculty in particular: "Practitioners and educators have the daunting task of trying to figure out how to foster motivation for the larger proportion of students that aren't active. Simply providing information on guidelines has not proven effective" (pp. 201–202). To resolve this problem, Beck and Diehr have turned to AST. After all, their goal was for students to internalize the fitness activities covered by the course.

Following AST protocol, Beck invited his 136 students to participate in determining the definitions of the most significant fitness concepts for the course. For example, instead of providing students with definitions of cardiorespiratory fitness and muscular strength for students to commit to memory, Beck asked his students to give examples of the exercise that they were already doing—whether this was walking along the fence line to examine it for repairs, hiking up flights of stairs, or taking the dogs around the block. These exercises were gathered and organized under each fitness concept. Once all concepts had been defined by students in this way, they had no trouble designing their own exercise routines with little assistance.

In pre- and postintervention scores, Beck and Diehr found small but significant increases in students' perceived fitness competence and perceived autonomous motivation. In their conclusion, they share the following advice for instructors who teach general education or other mandatory fitness courses: "If instructors taught in an autonomy-supportive manner, students might not only gain the knowledge required of the course, but they might also increase their motivation to partake in physical activity. That increased motivation could, in turn, have long-lasting health benefits to students" (p. 205).

REMEDIAL WRITING COURSES

At my university, it is a common gripe that students struggle with their writing. My school is an access institution, which means that students may be admitted even if they do not meet basic high school writing standards. These students are required to take remedial writing courses, which are designed to help them bridge the gap in their writing skills. The remedial courses must be completed successfully before those students are permitted to begin taking their college-level writing courses. For students entering college with little academic preparation, there is a lot riding on the success of these remedial courses. Thankfully, AST is helpful for students in this circumstance.

At a minority-serving community college in the United States, researchers found that students in remedial and entry-level writing courses benefited from autonomy support (Villarreal & García, 2016). The authors interviewed 18 male students of color in order to get a better idea of the factors that helped predict student achievement, determination, and success in remedial courses. Three themes emerged: (1) students succeeded when course goals were viewed within the context of their personal academic goals, (2) successful students sought independent help from the faculty teaching these courses as well as the support staff, and (3) they relied on inner determination when course difficulty was great enough to consider withdrawing.

In other words, in the cases where students achieved despite the odds against them doing so, it was because these students felt supported by the English faculty and staff at their school. These resources were provided in a variety of formats (e.g., writing lab, office hours, tutoring), and students were most likely to use them when information about them was shared in class and they were invited to do so. The authors also recommended that autonomy and relatedness could be included as learning objectives for such courses.

MUSIC AND PERFORMING ARTS

Throughout my childhood, I trained as a classical pianist. I had many different piano teachers—Russian, Vietnamese, Dutch, and American—but they all had one thing in common: They were all unwaveringly strict. Playing the piano requires discipline—disciplined posture, disciplined fingering, disciplined practice. Therefore the best piano teachers were also strict disciplinarians.

Music and other performance fields require high levels of personal discipline, and they often have a long history of authoritarianism: the expert insists that the novice do as they are told.

For music faculty, this means that the very discipline that they teach requires a certain measure of control. Music faculty at University of Roehampton in London, UK, have described the situation. "Teachers," Bonneville-Roussy et al. (2020) write, "felt that the pressure and controlling attitudes came from the institutions," as well as from a long history of controlling instructional practices in nineteenth-century musical tradition specifically. But there is a problem with this history: neither music student nor music faculty feel like authoritarian instruction is a helpful way for teaching or learning musical performance.

In their qualitative study, Bonneville-Roussy and others collected comments from 190 music students and 35 music performance faculty. Among other relationships between instructor behavior and student motivational regulation, they found a positive correlation between the provision of choice (where students were given choices about curricula or activities) and the intention to pursue a career in musical performance. And they found a negative correlation between this intention and psychological control (manipulating students into behaviors by selectively giving/withholding attention and encouragement).

As an example of the sort of impact that autonomy-supportive teaching had on students, the authors share the following observation, taken from student 2,038 of their study: "My singing teacher, with her exercises, brings my voice to its best and most effortless state every time, and doesn't perceive any piece that I bring to her as impossible or not right for me now, even if it's ridiculously difficult" (p. 110). Some students, however, found that such provisions of choice were given unequally—that instructors were playing favorites with their students.

In summary, the authors observe that aspects of music performance instruction lend themselves to high levels of autonomy support. After all, instructors must take into consideration where their students are at and what skills they have in order to work with them (e.g., a vocal range will limit the musical selection). But this comes with a tradeoff. "Classical performance training has a long history of cultivating a culture of controlling teaching styles in music" (p. 98)—a culture that persists today in music classrooms.

My classical training on the piano ended abruptly at thirteen, when I was given the choice to stop. I wouldn't continue playing until a decade later, when I discovered the beautiful pieces written by Yann Tiersen and Ludovico Einaudi.

PSYCHOLOGY AND SOCIAL SCIENCES

In a study conducted using 91 undergraduate students at a university in the United States, Jang and others (2016) found that students whose instructors taught their course material in student-preferred ways perceived their instructors as more autonomy supportive than students whose instructors taught their courses in non-student-preferred ways. Their method for differentiating between the two provides a simple example of taking students' perspective.

Students in sections of a required educational psychology course were given the following list of teaching methods, and were asked to rate these methods in terms of their preference for material delivery:

- Listen to a Guest Speaker
- Listen to a Student Presentation
- Listen to a Lecture
- Listen to an Audio Clip
- Watch a Video Clip
- Engage in Independent Seatwork
- Participate in a Whole-Class Discussion
- Complete a Prepared Worksheet
- Participate in Cooperative Learning
- Complete a Drill-and-Practice Session

Methods that received the most votes were considered "student preferred," and those that received the fewest votes were considered "student nonpreferred." (In case you are curious, the most popular teaching style was "Listen to a Guest Speaker," which was followed closely behind by "Watch a Video Clip." The least popular styles were "Listen to a Student Presentation" and "Complete a Prepared Worksheet.")

Using the results of the survey, Jang and coresearchers designed two instructional interventions. In the first teaching condition, instructors used a pair of highly preferred teaching styles. In the second condition, instructors used a pair of nonpreferred teaching styles. As expected, students in the first condition had higher need satisfaction, greater conceptual learning, and even perceived their instructors as having greater expertise.

SCIENCES AND LIBERAL ARTS IN SOUTH AMERICA

Matos and others (2018) confirmed their hypothesis that students' perceptions of teacher autonomy support increased student behavioral engagement, emotional engagement, agentic engagement, and cognitive engagement in 336 Peruvian college students (262 students taking courses in the liberal arts, and 74 students taking courses in the sciences). Additionally, early semester student agentic engagement correlated positively with end-of-semester perceived autonomy support.

In a group of 498 Columbian university students, correlations were found between students' perceived autonomy support and student psychological needs satisfaction, intrinsic motivation, and life satisfaction (Lozano-Jiménez et al., 2021).

ARTS AND HUMANITIES, HEALTH SCIENCES, ENGINEERING, AND EXERCISE SCIENCES IN EUROPE

Over 1,000 Spanish university students who were completing courses in sport, exercise science, and psychology showed higher levels of life satisfaction and professional competence in autonomy-supportive classrooms (Hernández et al., 2022).

Researchers at a university in Barcelona found that autonomy-supportive teaching styles correlated negatively with student procrastination and positively with student psychological needs satisfaction (Codina et al., 2018). This relationship was reversed for students whose instructors used a controlling style. The correlations stood across 675 students, who represented fields of arts and humanities, health sciences, juridical and social sciences, and engineering.

ONLINE AND ASYNCHRONOUS COURSES

In her doctoral dissertation, Tammy McClain-Smith (2017) studied something with which she had some familiarity from her own courses: autonomy support in asynchronous online classes.

In asynchronous courses, students do not interact with their instructors in real time. Asynchronous classes can be set up as a series of modules that students complete on their own schedule. The courses can include video-recorded lectures, discussion boards, traditional deadlines and exams, and so on. As online education has grown, asynchronous courses have become more and more common.

McClain-Smith interviewed students about their experience in these asynchronous courses. She was trying to get a handle on what seemed to work in that space, and what did not. She learned, for example, that it was helpful when the instructor understood the learning management system. This might sound like an obvious advantage, but it is not uncommon for an instructor to be tossed, so to speak, into an online course without adequate training. Even with exhaustive training, failure to understand the importance or significance of an online classroom's features from the perspective of students will make the training obsolete. At least this has been my experience.

I have taught online courses for ten years—probably a grand total of around 50 courses. I have been fortunate to have had the same platform throughout the years, yet I am still learning how to best integrate its features for my students. Despite being trained on the system while in graduate school, it took me 18 months and five online courses before I realized that a so-called helpful feature had made it impossible for me to respond to student emails by using the "Reply" option. This was a simple fix once I understood it, but it required a lot of disrupted communications before I knew there was a problem at all! (Emails were being forwarded from the learning management software to my faculty email address, so my replies had nowhere to go.) I can share similar stories about posting feedback for discussions or written papers, posting course announcements, organizing quizzes and exams, creating web links, uploading photos or video, sending reminders, and on and on.

Examining her interviews, McClain-Smith also recognized that asynchronous students benefited from a detailed course outline and structure from the very beginning of the semester. This is in particular an advantage to nontraditional students—those who are often working (one or more) full-time jobs or taking care of children and family members. These students do not have the luxury of taking time off for their studies, but must add studying on top of their already busy schedules. When an instructor provides clear and unambiguous course expectations, the nontraditional student is able to make an adequate plan (arranging for extra family help, a babysitter, or making work schedule changes when necessary).

In her final analysis, McClain-Smith shares the following three main themes that were most helpful for nontraditional students who experienced autonomy support in their asynchronous online courses: support, personal relevance, and time.

In the support theme, students perceived that their instructors supported them by understanding their unique situation, providing additional help through feedback and corrections, keeping constant communication and encouragement, accommodating the course structure, showing enthusiasm, and understanding student frustration.

Students perceived the course as personally relevant when their instructor invited them to use personal experiences and materials of personal interest, and students were given a choice of topics and course format.

The time theme included instances where students were given flexibility on when to complete assignments (early or later), shortened meetings and consolidated schedules, and flexibility in methods and means of contacting instructors.

GRADUATE SCHOOL

As mentioned earlier, faculty at a Canadian medical school (Neufield & Malin, 2020) found that autonomy-supportive instructional practices were positively correlated with medical students' perceived competence satisfaction (students felt like they were learning), relatedness satisfaction (they felt connected to others), and psychological well-being. AST practices were negatively correlated with students' perceived autonomy frustration, competence frustration, and relatedness frustration. All correlations were statistically significant ($p < 0.01$).

GENDER DIFFERENCES IN HIGHLY SPECIFIC CASES

Gender differences may moderate the impact of autonomy-supportive teaching in very specific cases. This has been found with Chinese students, where collectivist cultural norms indicate that college students are less expected to become autonomous from their families than with college students from individualistic cultures (Ma et al., 2020). When courses were consistent with student interests (e.g., courses were in a students' career field), autonomy support was positively correlated with social competence. When courses were not consistent with student interests, then this positive correlation was only found in female students. The authors explained this difference by looking at differences in how Chinese boys and girls are raised. That is, "males are expected to persist with effort in the face of difficulties, and to solve these challenges tenaciously" (p. 4).

Intercultural and International Applicability

Evidence shows that autonomy-supportive teaching works in colleges and universities irrespective of culture, nationality, ethnicity, gender, and socioeconomic category.

In general, instructional practices vary by nation and culture. Instructors from cultures that emphasize egalitarianism, for example, have a higher autonomy-supportive motivational baseline than instructors from cultures that emphasize authoritarianism. When instructors practice autonomy-supportive teaching, however, these cultural and national differences begin to disappear. When comparing controlling teaching styles, nationality explains 8.4% of the variance. When comparing autonomy-supportive styles, nationality explains only 3.1% (Reeve et al., 2014).

Reeve and Cheon (2021) conducted an exhaustive literature review of over 50 experiments and quasi-experiments that spanned K–12 teachers, college professors, and coaches of professional athletes in 17 countries and across five continents, all of which supported the claims that (1) autonomy-supportive teaching is something that can be learned by educators, and (2) autonomy-supportive teaching is beneficial to students. This means that, in the majority of instruments used across the more than fifty cases, instructors were effectively trained to use autonomy-supportive strategies, and their students benefited from the new autonomy-supportive practices. The most significant national difference was the likelihood that faculty will participate in professional development! The authors write, "teachers in China, Singapore, and Korea, for instance, are generally passionate about professional development, while teachers in some other nations take a less enthusiastic attitude toward these same opportunities" (p. 69). (The authors are careful not to specify which countries.)

Minority students in particular benefit from teaching that is autonomy supportive. This is because the curriculum often ignores who they are as individuals, ignores their cultural differences, and is often designed to transform the minority student into something other than who they are. American urban educator Chris Emdin (2016) describes this educational process as the erasing of indigenous and neo-indigenous cultures. This means that the very practice of learning asks students to alienate themselves from their families and ancestry. What Emdin suggests to reverse this process of alienation is what he calls reality pedagogy, which begins with taking students' perspective. He specifically recommends that instructors meet students where they are; that they invite students to participate in designing features of the course and to give feedback about instructor practices; that instructors focus on more than information in the classroom, but to focus also on the soul of those who are present; that instructors acknowledge all sorts of classroom participation without privileging convention or obedience for their own sake; and so on. In short, Emdin advocates supporting students' autonomy.

Evidence suggests that minority students are badly in need of instructors who support their basic psychological needs. Bunce and King (2019) interviewed 17 self-identified black and minority women about their experiences with autonomy support at a university in the United Kingdom. The reports were grim. The authors write, "most students spoke of how they experienced a significant lack of autonomy in the learning and teaching environment," which included the use of material that seemed irrelevant for the minority students and that "did not tackle the challenging issues of diversity and inclusion that they [the students] faced on a regular basis" (p. 4). The following student comment communicates this perfectly, right down to the syntax:

> We don't really sit down to talk about [diversity] . . . we've never . . . we haven't talked about this. . . . At first, I thought do I really want to go to this [research group]? . . . It always feels like you're putting yourself in the spotlight, of being attacked. . . . So it's a case of shall I be quiet and endure it, or . . . shall I speak up? (Participant 7; in Bunce & King, 2019, p. 4)

Bunce and King have a similar recommendation to that of Emdin: "Lecturers must recognize the importance of discussing different perspectives in class, play an active role in encouraging [black and minority] students to share their views and experiences, and give positive stimulating feedback" (p. 6). Furthermore, instructors "are in an optimal position to introduce and co-create new content with [black and minority] students to achieve diversity in the curriculum, and enable students to create project and assessment topics that they consider to be personally relevant" (p. 6).

In their recommendation about culturally responsive teaching, Reeve and Cheon (2021) share how "teacher participation in an autonomy-supportive intervention may be a helpful catalyst to incorporate culturally-informed, responsive, sensitive, and relevant teaching recommendations" (p. 70).

Conclusion

During the review stage, one of the readers suggested that AST only worked in primary and secondary school—that it had never been successfully applied to higher education. I spent too long puzzling over why this might be, and wondering how I could be the one to initiate it. As I explained in the book's introduction, I had experienced the benefits firsthand and believed them to be a consequence of AST.

Eventually I stopped puzzling and began looking for evidence that AST could be applied to higher education. As you can see, it has. There is still room for improvement, of course, particularly in the online spaces. But the accumulating evidence makes a strong case for any college professors or faculty development specialists or deans or chairs who are wondering about how to better support students in their learning.

Part II

APPLICATION

CHAPTER 4

Self-Determination Theory Workshop

The workshop activities in this and in the following chapters are intended to provide a general introduction to the application of SDT and AST into the college and university classroom. The specific details around each of the activities could easily be adjusted to meet the reality of a specific instructor or a specific department or program. The examples that I provide have come from a workshop that was organized in the United States and at a minority-serving public university.

In my first faculty workshop, I did not spend any time introducing my colleagues to Self-Determination Theory. This was a mistake. Without understanding the psychology of motivation upon which it is based, the AST strategies seem like nothing more than helpful teaching practices. Consequently, motivational changes were ignored.

Wishing to avoid that oversight in this book, I have created a graduated series of reflection questions designed to introduce a college instructor to autonomy support (and lack thereof) in their own work, and then to consider the same kinds of motivational mechanics as experienced by students. The questions in this chapter stem from the concepts that were introduced in chapter 1. They are accompanied by a short description that makes this connection.

As with all personal and professional development activities, the following questions are best answered from a place of quiet reflection and humility. They are opportunities to examine your own assumptions and to take seriously the impact that your perspective has on your students. All of this requires patience.

Basic Psychological Needs

SDT researchers have identified three basic psychological needs that, when met, lead to thriving and flourishing. These are autonomy, competence, and relatedness. The following open-ended questions are your opportunity to reflect on these basic psychological needs as they are supported or thwarted in your daily life:

1. Describe a recent time in your job when you felt micromanaged (e.g., by a department chair, college dean, regional accrediting agency, etc.). *[This is an example of what it feels like to be controlled.]*
2. Describe a time when you were given a task to complete, but nobody ever followed up with you (or the task changed without your input). *[This is an example of what it feels like to be in a chaotic or laissez-faire work environment.]*
3. Identify a part of your job that you enjoy so much that you would do it (or that you actually do it) for free. Did you always feel this way, or does this reflect a change in your interests and priorities? *[This is an example of intrinsic motivation.]*
4. Describe a time when you were assigned a task to do, but were given flexibility with how you could do it. *[This is an example of choice, which allows you to be self-determined despite having been given a job to do. The SDT word for this is "internalization."]*
5. Describe a time when somebody at your school helped you do something that you wouldn't have been able to do on your own. What was it about others that made them helpful to you? How were they able to do this? *[Here you are asked to analyze a time your autonomy was supported for an intrinsically regulated behavior.]*
6. Identify a skill of yours that you are proud of. Have you always been good at this skill, or have you worked at it? *[This question explores the difference between fixed- and growth-mindsets. It also demonstrates the importance of competence.]*
7. Describe a time when you gave up on a project or task that you had started because it was too difficult. *[This question demonstrates the importance of competence by demonstrating what happens when it is thwarted.]*
8. Have you ever felt lonely in aspects of your job? What were you doing, and how did that feel? *[This question demonstrates the importance of relatedness by demonstrating what happens when it is thwarted.]*
9. Describe a time when you felt connected to others in your job (e.g., with students, colleagues, coresearchers, etc.). *[This demonstrates the importance of relatedness.]*
10. Think of the best or one of the best experiences you have had in your career. Identify how each of the following factors contributed to that experience (if at all):

    a. Autonomy
    b. Competence
    c. Relatedness

Now it is time to think about your students.

1. Describe a situation where students might feel micromanaged by something their instructor has asked them to do. *[In which ways do you or other instructors control students?]*
2. Describe a real or imagined circumstance in which students feel confused by what they are expected to do for a class. *[In which ways do you or other instructors create chaotic or laissez-faire learning environments?]*

3. Imagine a situation where students are able to solve an important classroom problem with the help of their instructor. *[This question describes a situation where students can practice self-determined choice despite being given a task to do. By anticipating the students' needs, the instructor further supports students' autonomy.]*

4. Have you ever noticed when students are proud of what they have done or what they can do? Describe one such situation. What was the skill? Do you imagine that this was something that they worked on, or something that they were born with the ability to do? *[This question demonstrates the role and importance of competence in student classroom behavior.]*

5. Describe a classroom situation in which students might feel alienated or isolated from others. Now describe a classroom situation in which they feel connected to others. *[This question demonstrates the role and importance of relatedness for students in the classroom.]*

6. ADVANCED: Answer each of the questions using actual examples from your own classrooms. *[This question requires that the instructor be honest about the classroom environment that they create for their students. Watching a recording of yourself can be a useful practice for answering this question honestly.]*

By answering these questions honestly and candidly, you have examined the ways in which your own psychological needs have been supported and thwarted, and, if you have analyzed these experiences closely, then you have probably also noticed how your mood and feelings were affected. You have also adopted the perspective of students and have creatively imagined (or attempted to identify) instances where students' psychological needs are supported or thwarted.

Regulation of Beliefs, Values, and Behaviors

Now that we have explored the three basic psychological needs from our own perspectives and from the perspective of our students, we can move onto the SDT mini-theory of internalization. This begins by recognizing the many forms of regulation.

Our beliefs, values, and behaviors can be regulated a number of ways. They can be completely self-regulated (intrinsic) or completely unregulated (amotivation or no regulation). And there are four types of regulation in between: external, introjected, identified, integrated. Here they are once more:

No Regulation: Absence of activity, behavior, interest, or concern.

External Regulation: Beliefs, values, and behaviors are regulated by external demands, generally taking the forms of reinforcement and/or punishment.

Introjected Regulation: A person seems to be self-directed, but they are actually following rules that they have learned such as, "Good students never miss class." Because these rules have come from external sources, the behavioral regulation is still understood to be mostly external.

Identified Regulation: A person begins to be self-regulating. External beliefs, values, and behaviors are adopted by the student, but the student does not have to change their existing beliefs, values, and behaviors in order to adopt the new ones.

Integrated Regulation: A student begins to amend their existing beliefs, values, and behaviors in order to accommodate new ones, which they accept wholeheartedly.

Intrinsic Regulation: A student is wholly driven by self-direction. Beliefs, values, and behaviors well up from within the student.

1. Describe a job-related task that you decided wasn't worth your interest or time, so you decided not to do it. *[This is an example of No Regulation.]*
2. Describe a job-related task that you weren't interested in, but the incentive was attractive enough for you to complete it anyhow. *[External regulation.]*
3. Finish the sentences: "Good professors always . . ." "Good professors never . . ." For each sentence you completed, what do you imagine is the consequence for professors who have violated your rules? *[The completed sentences help identify the introjected beliefs an instructor has about good teaching.]*
4. Are there any parts of your job that you didn't initially enjoy, but, over time, have learned to gain satisfaction from? If so, what are those parts? What is it about yourself that led to a change in perspective? *[This question helps an instructor identify activities that have become internalized. More specifically, the activity has become Identified.]*
5. Have any of your personal or occupational beliefs or values undergone a substantial transformation? How would you describe that change? *[Assuming the belief or value came from somewhere, this question demonstrates Integrated regulation of, in this case, a belief or value.]*
6. Which aspect of your job do you love the most? (You are allowed to say "compensation," if you'd like). How does this aspect support your personal goals? *[This question demonstrates Intrinsic Regulation.]*

Now that we have some personal familiarity with external and internal regulation, as well as how something external can become internalized, it is time to shift our focus to students.

7. What sort of evidence might you look for to determine that students find class attendance and participation to be a waste of their time? *[No regulation of student behavior, beliefs, and values.]*
8. What external reinforcements do faculty at your school rely on to get students to engage in course material and do their work? *[External regulation of student behavior.]*
9. What beliefs do your students have about what makes the best college student? Finish the sentences: "The best college students always . . ." and "The best college students never . . ." *[This question demonstrates students' introjected behaviors, beliefs, and values.]*
10. How might a college instructor compel their students to complete an activity by relying on introjected regulation? *[This question demonstrates just how easy it is for instructors to exploit student introjection.]*
11. What is it about your discipline or the courses that you teach that students find interesting? Dull? *[For an instructor, this is the beginning of taking your students'*

perspective. It helps identify those aspects of a course that are most/least likely to become internalized by students.]

12. What beliefs and values do your students have that are at odds with the beliefs and values of your discipline or the material covered in your courses? (E.g., do religious beliefs conflict with scientific beliefs?) *[This question helps investigate discipline-specific values and behaviors that may be difficult for students to internalize.]*

13. Describe what it might look like for a student to adopt a new value that does not come into conflict with their existing beliefs and values. *[This question helps identify discipline-specific values or behaviors that would be simple for students to internalize.]*

14. Describe a real or imagined student whose beliefs or values have changed significantly during the semester. (This can be with respect to a topic or discipline, or about learning more generally.) What was it about this student that allowed them to change their perspective? What was it about this student's environment that may have played a role in this change? *[The first question helps identify what Integrated Regulation might look like. The following questions examine the conditions that made this possible.]*

In this series of questions, you have been asked to imagine and predict how students' psychological needs are supported and thwarted and the factors that lead to internal/external behavioral regulation. Once you feel confident in your understanding of the relationship between the environment and a person's psychological needs and behavioral regulation, then the next step is to practice observing this relationship as it is occurring. This means noticing how, for example, the way you welcome students into the classroom impacts their psychological needs satisfaction and shapes their behavioral regulation. It is extremely powerful to witness this impact in person, especially when you can make changes to your own behavior in response to what students are showing you (whether or not they are aware of it). To help develop this skill, I recommend recording class periods and then rewatching them, paying special attention to moments were enthusiasm and morale seem low or high.

After completing this first workshop, an instructor will have a good idea about how the strategies described in the previous chapters might produce the kinds of changes they have been shown to produce. I am also confident that the instructor will already begin to see that there is a lot more at stake in the virtual or face-to-face classrooms than course learning objectives. This something more is psychological well-being, and, for students, this is the difference between feeling fulfilled by their coursework, and simply doing as they're told.

CHAPTER 5

Diagnosing Teaching Styles with AST Inventories

A neat feature of autonomy-supportive teaching is that it comes with an assortment of assessments, surveys, questionnaires, observation forms, and other data collection instruments that have been validated. In this chapter, I provide those instruments and give instructions for using them.

By beginning your AST practice with a few inventories, you will be able to diagnose existing problems and anticipate areas for improvement. This chapter includes three well-known and commonly used inventories. The first is called the situations in school inventory (SIS, Aelterman et al., 2019), which is a self-report inventory that the instructor takes. The SIS asks the instructor to reflect on their own teaching practices. The second is called the learning climate questionnaire (Williams et al., 1994), which is a self-report inventory that students take. The learning climate questionnaire asks students to reflect on the autonomy support provided by their instructor. The final inventory is an observation form (Reeve, 2016), and it may be filled out by a fellow instructor, administrator, or researcher who is visiting the classroom of another instructor. The observation form asks the visitor to reflect on the climate provided by the instructor whose classroom they are visiting.

A Preliminary Note on the Difference Between Assessment and Evaluation

There is an important difference between assessment and evaluation when it comes to education research. Both are actions that begin with the collection and analysis of data. But their uses are very different.

Assessment belongs to a process of continuous program improvement, and it is generally what is called for by regional accrediting agencies. With assessment, data is useful only insofar as it reveals where and how improvements might be made. As you can imagine, all sorts of data are potentially useful for the purposes of assessment. In the classroom, this could include teacher observations, student observations, tests scores, measures of student engagement, measures of student creativity, visitor observation forms, and so on. There is no end to the types of data that could, when considered creatively, be useful for examining a range of possible outcomes.

Evaluation, by comparison, belongs to experimentation and hypothesis testing. The evaluator is less interested in the question, "how can I make this better?" Instead the evaluator asks, "does it work?" In order to conduct an evaluation, experimental control is very important. The evaluator wants to be able to test whether or not a new teaching strategy has been responsible for a change. For evaluations to be successful, changes have to be introduced incrementally and with care and precision. Strategies for sampling, data collection, and data analysis are all important to the evaluator. Because there is always a probability that what happens inside a given classroom does not represent what might happen in all classrooms, it is also helpful for evaluators to conduct significance tests, such as a *t*-test for a single variable or an analysis of variance for multiple variables. These techniques allow an evaluation of one classroom to be generalized to many classrooms.

Autonomy-supportive teaching can be assessed or evaluated. Which strategy you choose will depend on your goals. If you are interested in improving how supported your students feel, then a formal or informal data collection can be useful to see whether you are on the right track. If you are interested in seeing whether AST improves learning outcomes, then you might conduct a controlled study where one class is conducted using AST and another is conducted without using AST. The outcomes between both classes can then be compared to see whether the variable of AST was impactful, and if this impact was statistically significant.

In my teaching, I have used both. I have conducted a controlled quasi-experiment (it was quasi-experimental because I did not sample using random assignment) on the effectiveness of AST in promoting students' perceived autonomy support in an online course (this is shared in chapter 9). Because the difference in means was so small, the statistical findings were not helpful. But I also collected a variety of other data sets without controlling for variables, and these other sources of data were useful for finding areas for improvement in my teaching that I hadn't previously considered.

In what follows, I introduce the AST instruments, which can be used for assessment or evaluation. I am particularly interested in their use as tools of assessment, but I know that the institute of research and evaluation at my school is particularly interested in their use as tools of evaluation. Use them however you wish.

Situations in School Inventory

The situations in school (SIS) inventory (Aelterman et al., 2019) is a self-report questionnaire where the instructor is asked to reflect on the classroom climate they provide for their students. Classroom climate can be used in a variety of ways, but the authors of the inventory have in mind a very specific definition of classroom climate: it is the degree to which a teacher provides structure, chaos, autonomy support, and control in their classrooms. True to its name, the inventory asks teachers to consider 15 typical situations that occur in the classroom. If you have done the math, then you will see that the entire inventory requires 60 responses.

Because it is a self-report questionnaire, the SIS inventory is most useful as a tool for a teacher's self-reflection and self-assessment. It would make a poor evaluation tool, because it would be very easy to manipulate the results in whichever direction might be desirable. To that end, it is recommended that the SIS inventory only be used if an instructor is interested in genuine and honest self-disclosure. It is only helpful if the instructor is willing to be transparent, at least in the privacy of their own self-assessment.

ASSESSING STRUCTURE

As it is described throughout this book, the structure an instructor provides refers to how clear the assignments, activities, requirements, and learning objectives are to students, as well as how consistent and organized the course seems to students. Examples of structure include providing students with a schedule that specifies when the exams will take place, or outlining in a syllabus or course plan what the attendance policy will be.

When offered in an autonomy-supportive way, structure leads to greater internalization, and it leads to psychological need satisfaction. This is because structure makes clear to students the boundaries of the course within which they can stretch out and practice their autonomy.

ASSESSING CHAOS

Chaotic courses are unpredictable. Students are always unsure of what is expected of them each day, so they become overly cautious or disengaged. An extreme example of this would be the teacher who gives surprise quizzes frequently, or who cancels class without telling anybody. Students eventually learn that it is impossible to prepare for the class. Students in a chaotic course will not know whether there is an attendance policy, and, if so, what that attendance policy is. Students might know that there will be four exams, for example, but they won't know when those exams will be.

ASSESSING AUTONOMY SUPPORT

Supporting student autonomy has been the main feature of this book. If you have reached this chapter, then you could probably design useful questions that ask how supportive an instructor is of their students' autonomy.

In this classroom climate inventory, Aelterman and others clarify that by autonomy support they mean that an instructor is attuned to their students, and the instructor invites student participation. By "attunement," the authors are referring to the degree to which an instructor is in sync with students—that is, how sensitive the instructor is to changes in affect, desire, and engagement in their students. If an instructor is attuned to their students, then they will notice when students become bored, indifferent, or overwhelmed.

By participation, the authors refer to the degree to which the instructor invites students to give feedback, shape the course, make decisions, interact with each other, and so on. Participation looks at how likely it is that students will be invited off of the sidelines, so to speak.

ASSESSING CONTROL

Control, as it was described in the introduction, is where the conventional teacher is most at home. A controlling teacher says, "this is how it will be, and you must all fall in line with my way of thinking." Controlling teachers use promises of rewards and threats of punishment to manipulate students into behaving in specific and predetermined ways. They are dismissive to students, and they are unattuned to student affect.

COMPLETING THE INVENTORY AND ANALYZING THE RESULTS

The inventory is divided into 15 situations, and each situation has four possible responses. The teacher is asked to consider each response, and to rate them using a Likert scale the degree to which that response represents what they have actually done in that same situation in their courses. For example, in situation 14, a few students have repeatedly failed your course. What do you do? Do you . . . insist that they try harder or threaten them with consequences? Choose "1" if this is never what you would do. Choose "7" if this is exactly what you would do.

And so on. This specific response looks at how controlling a teacher is.

Once the inventory has been completed, you can go back through all of the situations and add up the values you selected for structure, chaos, autonomy support, and control. You will wind up with four scores. Following the literature of AST, the most desirable teacher-student outcomes occur when a teacher is high on autonomy support and structure, and low on control and chaos.

The complete SIS inventory is provided next. It has, however, been adjusted from its original format in the appendix of Aelterman et al. (2019). If you wish to use the original inventory and therefore benefit from the validity testing it provides, then you are advised to look up the original inventory. The format provided here simplifies the scoring procedure for the purposes of ease. For example, instead of randomizing the order of item responses, the same order has been used for all questions such that all "a" responses represent structure, "b" responses represent "chaos," "c" responses represent "autonomy support," and "d" responses represent "control." That is,

a. Structure
b. Chaos
c. Autonomy support
d. Control

Once again, this organizational scheme is unhelpful if you are using the SIS inventory as an evaluation, because it makes it very obvious which options are the good options. However, if the teacher is interested in using it as a self-assessment, which is how I recommend it be used, then the organizational scheme here makes it easy to design a spreadsheet to score the responses automatically.

Situations in School Inventory

1. **Situation: Classroom rules.** You are thinking about classroom policies, so you

   a. make an announcement about your expectations and standards for being a cooperative student.

   $$1 \quad\quad 2 \quad\quad 3 \quad\quad 4 \quad\quad 5 \quad\quad 6 \quad\quad 7$$

   b. don't worry too much about the policies and regulations.

   $$1 \quad\quad 2 \quad\quad 3 \quad\quad 4 \quad\quad 5 \quad\quad 6 \quad\quad 7$$

   c. invite students to suggest a set of guidelines that will help them to feel comfortable in class.

   $$1 \quad\quad 2 \quad\quad 3 \quad\quad 4 \quad\quad 5 \quad\quad 6 \quad\quad 7$$

   d. post your policies. Tell students they have to follow all the policies. Post sanctions for disobeying the policies.

   $$1 \quad\quad 2 \quad\quad 3 \quad\quad 4 \quad\quad 5 \quad\quad 6 \quad\quad 7$$

2. **Situation: Lesson plan.** As you prepare for class, you create a lesson plan. Your top priority would be to

   a. communicate which learning goals you expect students to accomplish by the end of the lesson.

   $$1 \quad\quad 2 \quad\quad 3 \quad\quad 4 \quad\quad 5 \quad\quad 6 \quad\quad 7$$

   b. don't plan or organize too much. The lesson will unfold itself.

   $$1 \quad\quad 2 \quad\quad 3 \quad\quad 4 \quad\quad 5 \quad\quad 6 \quad\quad 7$$

   c. offer a very interesting, highly engaging lesson.

   $$1 \quad\quad 2 \quad\quad 3 \quad\quad 4 \quad\quad 5 \quad\quad 6 \quad\quad 7$$

   d. insist that students have to finish all their required work—no exceptions or excuses.

   $$1 \quad\quad 2 \quad\quad 3 \quad\quad 4 \quad\quad 5 \quad\quad 6 \quad\quad 7$$

3. **Situation: Starting class.** The class period begins, so you

   a. provide a clear, step-by-step schedule and overview for the class period.

          1   2   3   4   5   6   7

   b. don't plan too much. Instead, take things as they come.

          1   2   3   4   5   6   7

   c. ask students what they are interested to know about the learning topic.

          1   2   3   4   5   6   7

   d. insist firmly that students must learn what they are taught. Your duty is to teach; their duty is to learn.

          1   2   3   4   5   6   7

4. **Situation: Motivating students.** You would like to motivate students during class, so you decide to

   a. offer help and guidance.

          1   2   3   4   5   6   7

   b. minimize the lesson plan; let what happens happen in the lesson.

          1   2   3   4   5   6   7

   c. identify the personal benefits of the course activities and/or learning material.

          1   2   3   4   5   6   7

   d. pound the lectern and say loudly, "Now it is time to pay attention!"

          1   2   3   4   5   6   7

5. **Situation: Nonresponsive students.** You ask your students a challenging but do-able question to involve them in the lesson. As during the previous class period, however, you get only silence, so you

   a. clarify and reframe the question so that students can answer it.

          1   2   3   4   5   6   7

   b. sigh, give the answer, and move on.

          1   2   3   4   5   6   7

   c. ask students to discuss the question with their neighbor and then invite them to share their answer within their groups.

          1   2   3   4   5   6   7

   d. name a student who has to answer the question.

          1   2   3   4   5   6   7

6. **Situation: Student complaints.** At a difficult point in the lesson, students begin to complain. In response, you

   a. show and teach them a helpful strategy for how to break down the problem to solve it step by step.

      1   2   3   4   5   6   7

   b. just ignore the whining and complaining. They need to learn to get over the obstacles themselves.

      1   2   3   4   5   6   7

   c. accept their negative feelings as okay. Assure them that you are open to their input and suggestions.

      1   2   3   4   5   6   7

   d. insist they pay attention. They must learn this material for their own good.

      1   2   3   4   5   6   7

7. **Situation: Needing extra effort.** You present a difficult lesson that requires a lot of effort from students. In doing so, you

   a. say, "Because this lesson is extra difficult, I will provide you with extra help and extra assistance if you need it."

      1   2   3   4   5   6   7

   b. aren't too concerned, as students need to figure out for themselves how much effort to put forth.

      1   2   3   4   5   6   7

   c. try to find ways to make the lesson more interesting and enjoyable for your students.

      1   2   3   4   5   6   7

   d. insist firmly that "now is the time for hard work."

      1   2   3   4   5   6   7

8. **Situation: Anxiety surfaces.** During a class assignment, you notice that some students are showing signs of anxiety. You

   a. break down the steps needed to handle the assigned task so that students feel more capable of mastering it.

      1   2   3   4   5   6   7

   b. don't worry about it; let it pass on its own.

      1   2   3   4   5   6   7

   c. acknowledge that they look anxious and stressed. Invite them to voice their sense of unease.

      1   2   3   4   5   6   7

   d. insist that they must act in a more mature way.

      1   2   3   4   5   6   7

9. **Situation: Transition to a new activity.** One learning activity ends, and another is about to begin. You

   a. monitor how well each student is able to make the transition to a new activity.

   1   2   3   4   5   6   7

   b. just start the new activity—maybe students will follow.

   1   2   3   4   5   6   7

   c. be patient; confirm that those who are still working hard may have the time needed to finish.

   1   2   3   4   5   6   7

   d. command the students to hurry and to finish the old activity.

   1   2   3   4   5   6   7

10. **Situation: Student misbehavior.** A couple of students have been rude and disruptive. To cope, you

    a. communicate the classroom expectations for cooperation and prosocial skill.

    1   2   3   4   5   6   7

    b. let it go, because it is too much of a pain to intervene.

    1   2   3   4   5   6   7

    c. explain the reasons for your classroom behavior expectations. Later talk to them individually, and listen carefully to how they see things.

    1   2   3   4   5   6   7

    d. command that they get back on task immediately, otherwise there will be consequences.

    1   2   3   4   5   6   7

11. **Situation: Practice time.** It is time for students to practice what they have learned. You

    a. explain the solution to one problem step by step, then guide their progress and improvement on follow-up problems.

    1   2   3   4   5   6   7

    b. decide to wait and see how learning evolves without planning for it.

    1   2   3   4   5   6   7

    c. ask students which kinds of practice problems they want to work on the most.

    1   2   3   4   5   6   7

    d. demand that it is time to work, whether they like to or not. Remind them that they will sometimes be required to work against their will.

    1   2   3   4   5   6   7

12. **Situation: Argumentative students.** As class ends, it comes to your attention that two students are arguing and offending each other. As the rest of the students leave the classroom, you ask the two to remain so that you can

  a. be clear about what the classroom guidelines and expectations are. You indicate what helpful and cooperative behavior looks like.

  1   2   3   4   5   6   7

  b. let them finish their argument if that is what they want.

  1   2   3   4   5   6   7

  c. take the arguing students aside, and describe briefly what you saw and ask for their suggestions about what to do.

  1   2   3   4   5   6   7

  d. tell them that they should be ashamed of their behavior, and that, if they continue, then there will be sanctions.

  1   2   3   4   5   6   7

13. **Situation: Test results.** You have finished scoring a test or exam. Several students scored low again, even though you paid extra attention to this material last week. You

  a. help students revise their wrong answers so they understand what went wrong and how to improve,

  1   2   3   4   5   6   7

  b. don't spend class time on the low-scoring students.

  1   2   3   4   5   6   7

  c. listen with patience and understanding to what the students say about their test performance.

  1   2   3   4   5   6   7

  d. insist that low scores are unacceptable to you. Tell students that they must score higher for their own good.

  1   2   3   4   5   6   7

14. **Situation: Remediation.** A student is going to fail your course. You

  a. re-explain the learning material step by step until they have mastered it better.

  1   2   3   4   5   6   7

  b. don't intervene, but wait until they ask for additional support themselves.

  1   2   3   4   5   6   7

  c. say, "Okay, where might we start? Do you have any suggestions?"

  1   2   3   4   5   6   7

  d. insist that they try harder, that they get it right, and that they be serious, or else there will be consequences.

  1   2   3   4   5   6   7

15. **Situation: Homework.** When assigning homework, you

    a. communicate what it involves to do the homework, and check that everyone understands.

        1   2   3   4   5   6   7

    b. let the homework speak for itself rather than overexplaining everything.

        1   2   3   4   5   6   7

    c. offer a number of different homework exercises (such as three), and ask students to pick from those options.

        1   2   3   4   5   6   7

    d. make it clear that the homework has to be done well, or else consequences will follow.

        1   2   3   4   5   6   7

Scoring:

    Structure (Add together letter "a" responses) _____

    Chaos (Add together all letter "b" responses) _____

    Autonomy Support (Add together all letter "c" responses) _____

    Control (Add together all letter "d" responses) _____

ADVANCED SCORING

Each of the four instructional styles has been further broken down into two forms by the inventory. For example, chaos can be represented by abandoning students and by waiting for students to take charge. If you are interested in the finer breakdown of these items, then use the following calculations.

Structure. *Guiding*: add together 4a, 5a, 6a, 7a, 8a, 9a, 13a, and 14a and divide by 8. *Clarifying*: add together 1a, 2a, 3a, 10a, 11a, 12a, and 15a and divide by 7.

Guiding: _____   *Clarifying:* _____

Chaos. *Abandoning*: add together 5b, 6b, 7b, 8b, 9b, 10b, 12b, 13b, 14b, and 15b and divide by 10. *Awaiting*: add together 1b, 2b, 3b, 4b, and 11b and divide by 5.

Abandoning: _____   *Awaiting:* _____

Autonomy Support. *Participative*: add together 1c, 5c, 11c, 14c, and 15c and divide by 5. *Attuning*: add together 2c, 3c, 4c, 6c, 7c, 8c, 9c, 10c, 12c, and 13c and divide by 10.

Participative: _____   *Attuning:* _____

Control. *Demanding*: add together 1d, 2d, 3d, 5d, 6d, 10d, 13d, and 15d and divide by 8. *Domineering*: add together 4d, 7d, 8d, 9d, 11d, 12d, and 14d and divide by 7.

Demanding: _____   *Domineering:* _____

Learning Climate Questionnaire

The second assessment tool is a self-report inventory that students take that asks them to reflect on how autonomy supportive their instructor seems to be. It is called the learning climate inventory, and it is considered by AST scholars and researchers to be a reliable measure of perceived autonomy support.

By itself, the effort a teacher takes to improve the autonomy support they provide their students is likely to lead to improvements in the classroom and improved morale for everybody involved. But it would be helpful to test whether or not students recognize a difference, or if they can identify instances where their autonomy is encouraged and supported. The learning climate inventory provides this opportunity. It has been designed using simple questions, such as, "I feel able to share my feelings with my instructor," and it gives students seven response options between, "I strongly disagree" and, "I strongly agree." This is much easier than asking six or seven year olds (or 17-year-olds) whether they feel like their autonomy is being supported.

The learning climate inventory is available in six-item and 15-item versions, and both are short enough and simple enough to be added to any course, or even to be given to all students in a department or school. The inventory can be given at any point during the course, provided the students have had enough time to interact with their teacher and develop their own opinions about how class has been going.

This inventory has been used hundreds of times in peer-reviewed research, which means that it comes with strong social validity. A teacher can have some confidence that the results are meaningful—that is, if the results indicate a high level of perceived autonomy, then there is a good chance that the teacher in question has been successful in supporting student autonomy.

This can be useful in a pre-/post-test design to see whether or not a change to instructional technique has resulted in a change in student perception and participation. It can also be used as a diagnostic tool to see which teachers in a department or school district have the most room for improvement in terms of supporting student autonomy (provided, of course, the department or school district desires such changes).

I have found the learning climate inventory to be easily integrated into learning management software (such as Blackboard, D2L, and so on), where it can be shared with hundreds of teachers or given to thousands of students. Because the inventory takes only a few minutes to complete, the ease of its transmission means a wealth of data is easily collected. (Note: Item 13 is reverse scored.)

1. I feel that my instructor provides me with choices and options.[1]

1	2	3	4	5	6	7
Strongly Agree			Neutral			Strongly Disagree

2. I feel understood by my instructor.

1	2	3	4	5	6	7
Strongly Agree			Neutral			Strongly Disagree

---

1. Original inventory is available free of charge at www.selfdeterminationtheory.org/learning-climate-questionnaire/.

3. I am able to be open with my instructor during class.

1	2	3	4	5	6	7
Strongly Agree			Neutral			Strongly Disagree

4. My instructor conveyed confidence in my ability to do well in the class.

1	2	3	4	5	6	7
Strongly Agree			Neutral			Strongly Disagree

5. I feel that my instructor accepts me.

1	2	3	4	5	6	7
Strongly Agree			Neutral			Strongly Disagree

6. My instructor made sure I really understood the goals of the class and what I need to do.

1	2	3	4	5	6	7
Strongly Agree			Neutral			Strongly Disagree

7. My instructor encouraged me to ask questions.

1	2	3	4	5	6	7
Strongly Agree			Neutral			Strongly Disagree

8. I feel a lot of trust in my instructor.

1	2	3	4	5	6	7
Strongly Agree			Neutral			Strongly Disagree

9. My instructor answers my questions fully and carefully.

1	2	3	4	5	6	7
Strongly Agree			Neutral			Strongly Disagree

10. My instructor listens to how I would like to do things.

1	2	3	4	5	6	7
Strongly Agree			Neutral			Strongly Disagree

11. My instructor handles people's emotions very well.

1	2	3	4	5	6	7
Strongly Agree			Neutral			Strongly Disagree

12. I feel that my instructor cares about me as a person.

1	2	3	4	5	6	7
Strongly Agree			Neutral			Strongly Disagree

13 I don't feel very good about the way my instructor talks to me.

1	2	3	4	5	6	7
Strongly Agree			Neutral		Strongly Disagree	

14. My instructor tries to understand how I see things before suggesting a new way to do things.

1	2	3	4	5	6	7
Strongly Agree			Neutral		Strongly Disagree	

15. I feel able to share my feelings with my instructor.

1	2	3	4	5	6	7
Strongly Agree			Neutral		Strongly Disagree	

Classroom Observation Checksheet

If a teacher wishes for more detailed feedback about how they are getting along with their support of student autonomy, then they might want to have a trained observer visit their classroom to take notes.

The classroom observation form is divided in two, with one section asking questions about autonomy support, and another section asking questions about control.

In another variation of classroom observation, a teacher might record one of their courses to rewatch at a later time. They can fill out the classroom observation form themselves.

In practice, I have not found the trained observer version to be helpful. It can be intimidating to have another instructor visit your classroom and then provide a report on areas in which the observed teacher could improve. This has all the features of control (of teachers), and few features of autonomy support.

It works much better when the observer visits a classroom, and then fills out the observation form along with the instructor who is being observed. When done this way, the observer acts more as a facilitator of the observed instructor's self-reflection. Having the observer there increases the accountability that self-reflection will actually occur, and the observer can also share insights about what they observed that the teacher might have forgotten or overlooked.

Autonomy Support:		*Never*			*Occasionally*			*Always*
Takes the students' perspective:	1	2	3	4	5	6	7	

- Invites, asks for, welcomes, and incorporates students' input
- Is "in sync" with students
- Is aware of students' needs, wants, goals, priorities, preferences, and emotions

	Never			*Occasionally*			*Always*
Vitalizes inner motivational resources:	1	2	3	4	5	6	7

- Piques curiosity; provides interesting learning activities
- Vitalizes and supports students' autonomy, competence, and relatedness
- Frames learning activities with students' intrinsic goals

	Never			*Occasionally*			*Always*
Provides explanatory rationale:	1	2	3	4	5	6	7

- Explains why; says "because . . ." or "the reason is . . ."
- Identifies the value, importance, benefit, use, and utility of a request

	Never			*Occasionally*			*Always*
Uses nonpressuring, informational language:	1	2	3	4	5	6	7

- Flexible, open-minded, responsive communication
- Provides choices, provides options
- Says "you may . . ." or "you might . . ."

	Never			*Occasionally*			*Always*
Acknowledges and accepts negative affect:	1	2	3	4	5	6	7

- Listens carefully, nondefensively, and with understanding
- Acknowledges negative affect
- Accepts complaints as valid

	Never			*Occasionally*			*Always*
Displays patience:	1	2	3	4	5	6	7

- Allows students to work at their own pace and in their own way
- Calmly waits for students' signals of initiative, input, and willingness

Control:	*Never*			*Occasionally*			*Always*
Takes only teacher's perspective:	1	2	3	4	5	6	7

- Attends to and prioritizes only the teacher's plans and needs
- Teacher is out of sync with students, unresponsive to students' signals
- Is unaware of students' needs, wants, goals, priorities, and emotions

	Never			*Occasionally*			*Always*
Introduces extrinsic motivators:	1	2	3	4	5	6	7

- Offers incentives, seeks compliance
- Gives consequences for desired and undesired behaviors
- Utters assignments, directives, and commands

	Never			*Occasionally*			*Always*
Neglects to provide	1	2	3	4	5	6	7

explanatory rationale:
- Gives directives without explanations
- Makes requests without explanations

Never

	Never			*Occasionally*			*Always*
Uses controlling,	1	2	3	4	5	6	7

pressuring language:
- Evaluative, critical, coercive, and inflexible
- Is prescriptive with requests ("You should . . ." or "You must . . ." and so on)
- Verbally and nonverbally pressuring (raises voice, points, pushes hard)

Never

	Never			*Occasionally*			*Always*
Counters and tries to change	1	2	3	4	5	6	7

negative affect:
- Counters and argues against students' negative affect, complaining, or bad attitude
- Tries to change negative affect into something more acceptable to the teacher

Never

	Never			*Occasionally*			*Always*
Displays impatience:	1	2	3	4	5	6	7

- Rushes student to produce a right answer or a desired behavior
- Intrudes into students' workspace (grabs away learning materials, says "here, let me do that for you")
- Communicates what is right and pushes students to reproduce it quickly

CHAPTER 6

Taking Students' Perspective

It is not unusual to hear that teachers and college professors have planned course topics, activities, and assessments around their students' perspective. These faculty often share observations such as, "My students like it when . . ." and then go on to describe an activity that they feel students would probably endorse if asked. For example, I have heard about how

- "students like controversial topics,"
- "students don't like homework over extended weekends,"
- "students like it when technology is integrated into the class,"
- "students like videos,"
- "students hate to read from a textbook,"
- "students like discussion posts," and
- "students resent click-through courses."

These observations are the beginning, and they demonstrate the importance of taking students' perspectives. But, by themselves, the observations take for granted that student engagement and student disengagement are representative of student interest level. To be sure, students may seem to prefer a YouTube video to an oral lecture, but there is no reason to limit your judgment of what students are thinking to watching how they act. It wouldn't take much longer to ask them directly about what they like, what they don't like, and how they think the course could be improved.

Therefore, in order to take student perspective taking to a deeper level, the following activities ask the instructor to conduct impromptu surveys, data collections, interviews, polls, and more. Feedback can be gathered at any point during a course. It can be taken right away before an aspect of the course has taken shape so that students get to have a say in course design. Feedback can be gathered during an activity to see how it is going, and whether any productive changes might be made. Or it can be gathered after an activity has run its course, which allows student perspective to join instructor perspective in making a decision about whether the activity should be repeated.

Feedback can also be gathered with respect to any dimension of the course—from the learning objectives through the final assessment process. Table 6.1 provides a wide range of sample strategies for taking students' perspectives. The suggestions are not

Table 6.1. Sample strategies for taking students' perspectives, organized by course aspect and placement

	Before	*During*	*After*
Learning objectives	Ask students to review the course description, discipline, and their personal goals, and to brainstorm what they perceive to be worthwhile objectives for a course.	Mid-course, distribute blank sheets of paper with the learning objective written at the top. Ask students to evaluate the importance of the objective, or to make any recommended changes.	Once the course has ended, ask students to evaluate the benefit of the course objectives, and to offer their advice for doing it differently the next time around.
Topics	In a city hall–type classroom forum, ask students to share out loud any topics within the course discipline that interest them. Record all suggestions. Organize a vote by a show of hands (or by creating an online poll) to determine the topics around which to organize class.	Let students decide whether a specific topic merits extra time in the course schedule, or if it is time to move on to something else.	Create a poll where students can rank the topics that were discussed during the semester. Give them room to leave additional comments.
Resources	Develop a list of the forms of resources you can provide, such as PDFs, library books, YouTube videos, podcasts, and guest speakers. Poll students about which kinds of resources are most desirable. If necessary, enlist students to help find useful resources within the chosen form (e.g., you might not know where to find blogs on topics like biochemistry).	Ask students about a particular reading or homework activity before they do it. See if they think it is the best resource to fulfill the objective. If not, see what they may suggest instead. (Note: This isn't a suggestion between something and nothing.)	After a reading or lecture or workshop, ask students for honest feedback. Create a system for anonymous feedback about any resource you have provided, but be specific about which resource you want them to give feedback for.

	Before	*During*	*After*
Deliverables	If your course requires that the students produce something tangible, then give them several options to choose between. The entire class can make the choice (for a common deliverable) or students can choose their own (e.g., essay, presentation, poster, exam, interview, and so on).	As students are working out the basics of their essay/presentation/poster, check with them to see if any changes might be made to the course requirement. Does the introduction seem too long? Should you cut the conclusion? Go for breadth over depth? The opposite?	The day a big assignment is due is a great time to get candid comments about the assignment. What was easy? What was hard? What did you enjoy? What did you wish we had spent more time doing?
Assessments	Let students decide who (teacher or student) will conduct the assessments, and upon what criteria students will be assessed.	As students have begun working on a substantial, graded activity, ask them what kind of feedback they would be most interested in having. For an essay, do they want their grammar checked? Word choice? Style? Format?	This is difficult, because the big assessments usually come at the very end of a course. Try to design a way to get feedback about the assessment process itself. Let students know that they will be evaluating their instructor for their final assignment. Give them a chance to comment on how useful they found the assessment component.

exhaustive, but are intended to get faculty thinking more creatively about how and when they might gather students' perspectives.

Methods for Getting Student Feedback

The following are strategies that I have used for soliciting student feedback about aspects of my courses, along with anything I have learned about using each strategy. I hope that these methods are merely the start, and that readers will develop their own creative and useful ways for getting students to share their secrets.

DISTRIBUTE SLIPS OF PAPER ASKING FOR ANONYMOUS SUGGESTIONS

This strategy has been taken from AST researcher Johnmarshall Reeve (2016), who suggests distributing 3×5 index cards with the words "Any suggestions" written on the top. The students are given plenty of time to write whatever is on their minds, but they are not required to write anything if they do not wish. All students are asked to turn their cards in, even if their cards are blank. That way nobody feels pressured to say something (and therefore write something they don't really mean), and nobody feels like their comment will be spotted because it's the only one returned.

Because I am too lazy to go to the store to purchase index cards, I typically use scrap paper from the printer, which I cut into squares using an industrial paper cutter. I put stacks of these little squares into a zipped plastic baggie (to avoid them littering my work bag), and keep them with me all the time. I bring them out in the following two scenarios:

1. Whenever I am trying out something new (such as a reading, rubric, or resource), and I am eager to hear if students think it is as cool as I do.
2. Whenever I feel like an activity did not go as I thought it should go. Rather than wallow in self-pity, I see if students were as disappointed as I was. I usually find that a somewhat small change could be made to improve the activity. For example, I often learn about how I did a poor job of describing the activity (i.e., it was chaotic). By spending more time describing the activity and clarifying student options, I can avoid having the same activity fall flat the next time I try it.

As I gather feedback, I begin to feel more in tune with how my students are doing. I start to sense their problems before they become serious problems. I actually begin to recognize when students are confused or frustrated or bored without having to ask.

HOLD AN OPEN TOWN HALL–TYPE FORUM

I have found that smaller classes (fewer than 40) often prefer to hear from everybody all at once. This works best when generating and discussing lists (such as choosing course topics, deliverables, or learning resources). Sometimes I am surprised when students ask to do impromptu votes by show of hands, even when I have created anonymous surveys and polls for them to take on their phones.

I once generated a list of 100 topics in a course in human development with the intention of spending all class period going through them. Before reaching the Ds in my list, students cut me off and started calling out the ones that were most interesting to them—items I hadn't yet gotten to such as sexual abuse, trauma, and personal finance.

CREATE A VIRTUAL SURVEY OR POLL

With the proliferation of online course platforms and supporting software, it has become easy to design surveys and polls. These can generally be set up to be anonymous, if masking the identities of students is important.

The surveys can be used in collaboration with any of the previous suggestions. A list of possible course objectives can be generated using the anonymous slips of paper method, and then these can be used to fill a survey.

For example, in a research methods course I created a list of 25 interesting (to them, I thought) methods along with a one-sentence description of each. They stared at the sheet for a few minutes, and I asked if they were ready to vote on which methods we would focus on that semester. After much hesitation, it became clear that students wanted more than a one-sentence description in order to make their decision. I asked, "Would you be interested in a mini lecture about each?" and they explained that they would. So that's what I did. It was one of the most productive discussions I can remember, because students were asking questions about each method to see if they understood what it did. After the discussion, students needed some time to think over their decision, so I created a poll where they could choose their favorite methods. We used the results of the poll to organize the rest of the semester.

When to Avoid Taking Students' Perspective

It is important as an instructor to seek feedback only when you are genuinely interested in learning your students' perspective. If you feel upset, or if you are frustrated with your students, then getting their feedback may not be helpful. This is because you might be tempted to read or listen to their comments defensively, and your students will quickly realize that you are not sincerely interested in what they have to share. If this is the case, then you might be better off doing a journal reflection about your expectations for the course. Eventually work your way back to your expectations for students, and how you feel like they have let you down (or whatever shape your frustrations have taken).

Put It into Practice

The following homework activities are useful if the AST workshop takes place during a semester where faculty can practice each of the strategies in their current courses. If the workshop takes place (or if you are reading this book) during a break or before the semester begins, then you might practice these in other areas of your life such as with your family and friends (of course, you probably won't want to hand a comment card to a person after a date).

HOMEWORK ACTIVITY #1: DISTRIBUTE COMMENT CARDS

This first homework activity requires no planning or prereflection. All you have to do is buy (or make) 3 × 5 index cards and distribute them to students at any time during a class period.

Step 1: Buy (or make) 3 × 5 cards.

Step 2: Distribute the cards to students with the instruction: "I am interested in hearing your perspective about how class has been going. You may comment on any aspect of the course that you wish, or you may turn the blank card back in to me. Do not share your name."

Step 3: Collect the cards and read them after class.

Hint: It is helpful to students if you ask for feedback about a specific part of class, such as the daily schedule or one of the readings. This is because students have learned that course policies are always inflexible. It is sort of like asking a prisoner about suggestions for their accommodations: What can they really say except for how their meal is served?

HOMEWORK ACTIVITY #2: SEEK CANDID REVIEWS ABOUT COURSE CONTENT

Reflect on the courses that you teach, and choose one aspect that you are unsure about. Maybe it is a reading that you have assigned, a rubric you are using, or a new learning objective the university board is pushing on everybody. Enlist the help of your students in making the final judgment.

Step 1: Choose an aspect of your course that you are unsure about.

Step 2: State your uncertainty with the aspect chosen in step 1 as clearly as you can. (This will upset the perception that everything that happens in the classroom is without blemish.)

Step 3: Ask students for their honest feedback.

Step 4: Ask questions if you are uncertain about what students are saying with their feedback.

Hint 1: Step 4 may seem unnecessary, but it has been my experience that students struggle to state their concerns as baldly or as clearly as we might hope. In a town hall–type forum, you can summarize back to students what you have heard them say, and then make corrections with their help until they are satisfied that you understand their feelings and what they are saying. This can also work in an anonymous format, provided you summarize your understanding to students during the next meeting. For example, it isn't terribly helpful if a student says, "The rubric was good." The follow-up discussion will allow you to ask them, "What about the rubric was helpful?" and "Could anything be done to make the rubric even better?"

Hint 2: Give students an opportunity to give feedback on the entire course (or a significant part of it) by asking them toward the end of a semester or school year.

HOMEWORK ACTIVITY #3: INVITE STUDENTS TO COMMENT ON THE LESSON PLAN FOR THE DAY

This final homework activity has been taken from Reeve (2016). To do it, you start by sharing what you have in store for the class on that day (which is AST step 3, "Providing Explanatory Rationale"), and then ask your students, "How does that sound?"

Step 1: Share with your students what you have in store for the day.

Step 2: Ask students if that sounds okay.

Step 3: Be willing to make changes in the event that students have suggestions for how to make it better.

Problems to Expect, and How to Deal with Them

STUDENTS HAVE NO FEEDBACK TO SHARE

There is a good chance that your class will be the first time where students were asked to give feedback. It is understandable that they will be skeptical. They will think that your invitation for their feedback is some sort of trap, and nobody wants to wind up hanging from a tree in a cargo net.

This may be unavoidable the first few times, especially if your students have come to expect a controlling or chaotic classroom experience. But if you have communicated your interest in supporting their autonomy in other ways—you have listened sympathetically to them, acknowledged and accepted their affect, and so on—then they will take the invitation up in the spirit in which it was given.

I have found that it is helpful to be as clear and as specific as possible about the kind of feedback you are interested in. For example, instead of saying, "Do you have any suggestions?" you might ask, "Is there any activity, were it added, that would make the class better?" or "What improvements might we make for our group work?"

STUDENTS DON'T SEEM TO BE INTERESTED IN THEIR OWN SUGGESTIONS

In this scenario, students have made suggestions, and you have done your best to implement those suggestions into the class. Nobody, however, seems to be interested in the change.

This happens regularly in my classes. In one memorable experience, a group of students spent two class periods creatively and imaginatively choosing topics to discuss.

Students voted on the topics they were most interested in, and we began with the topic that had received the highest number of votes. The topic was "psychology of money." I picked out two optional videos and two optional readings about the topic, and we would meet to discuss anything of interest to them. Because I had been learning about supporting student autonomy, I had prepared a structured assignment in the event that students were unsure of where to begin.

There followed one of the most mundane class periods of my life. It was as if students were surprised by the topic they had voted on during the previous week. I became defensive, and was eager to point out to them that it was their number one choice, hoping that the cognitive dissonance might eat at them.

In subsequent instances where students stared absently at their own suggestions, I have learned to interpret it through one of the following valences. Either

1. what interests them has changed,
2. I misunderstood the suggestion, or
3. They are still interested in the topic, but aren't sure how to begin.

Thankfully, there are solutions to each of these.

Just because spousal abuse seemed like an interesting topic to discuss on Monday doesn't mean that students will still find it interesting on Friday or the following Monday. That's okay. Learn from the experience, and try to avoid planning too far into the future. Perhaps it will work best to choose the next topic closer to the day that it will be discussed.

It is more likely, however, that I have misunderstood the suggestion. When students voted on "psychology of money," I interpreted that as would a middle-aged college professor. I was keen to emphasize things like expense ratios, index funds, and opportunity costs. I gasped aloud when a student admitted to saving her money in an envelope. And so on. In other words, I wasn't really addressing my students' needs or interests. In the event that students are unsure of where to begin, I have found that it is helpful to open class time by asking students what they perceive as the biggest problem with respect to the topic. This allows students to take the lead in the discussion, and it gives them a chance to clarify their own understanding. If they are still quiet, then I might offer up a few suggestions. "I imagine that you are interested in finding the lowest expense ratios, is that right? No? Hmm." And so on.

In retrospect, it would have been more helpful had I let students define what they understood as "the psychology of money," or at least let them point me in a general direction.

STUDENTS HAVE ONLY POSITIVE FEEDBACK TO SHARE

Many of my colleagues reported that the feedback they got was unhelpful—that students had little more to share than vague compliments.

Once again, it will be important to keep in mind that this might be the first time your students have been asked to give feedback to an instructor. In the example where students say nothing, maybe they have decided that your invitation is a poorly disguised trap. Or maybe the students have decided that your invitation for their feedback is nothing more than a low-key assignment. As with all low-key assignments with negligible value beyond the grade they might receive, students give teachers what they imagine teachers want: marshmallow compliments. They say, "class is going wonderfully," and "nothing could possibly make this class better," and "you shouldn't change a thing."

Though such comments are possibly encouraging to professors, they do little for the purpose of improving class. To prevent this outcome, I try to be as clear as possible about the kind of feedback I am after. For example, I have used the following prompt as an end-of-term invitation for suggestions:

> Please share any feedback you have for me about this course. Honesty is appreciated. Your suggestions are helpful to me, because I use them to make changes to course requirements, the resources that I provide, and my behavior. Any suggestions that you share will not be held against you, and they will not impact your grade.
>
> I keep a record of these responses. They are the most cherished artifacts of my time as a teacher. I get warm and fuzzy feelings when the comments are generous or kind, but I learn more when the comments are critical or when constructive suggestions are made.

CHAPTER 7

Intrinsic Motivation

AST Strategy Two: Invite Students to Pursue Their Interests

The second strategy for supporting student autonomy is to invite students to make choices about course materials, topics, learning outcomes, and activities. This open invitation allows students to become intrinsically regulated. Many such examples have already been provided in table 6.1.

It is important to remember that this invitation must be real. The invitation to choose the first course topic doesn't count if you steer the conversation toward the topic you would really like to begin with.

Of all the strategies, this is the one in which students get to practice freedom along with autonomy. Psychologists recognize that freedom and autonomy, though related, are not synonyms. Freedom is the complete openness of possibility, and the only options for students are intrinsic regulation or no regulation. With autonomy, a person can choose to be externally regulated (which can be accomplished in a controlling or an autonomy-supportive way). Therefore, when inviting students to pursue their interests, one of their responses might be to sit quietly and wait for directions from you, their instructor. As their instructor, you can practice patience by waiting, and you can acknowledge their uncertainty and confusion. But, if they are still unwilling to share their interests, then you might have to provide direction, such as providing them with options.

In my experience, the biggest problem that an instructor will face with this strategy is a classroom full of quiet students. It is easy to become frustrated by indifference when students balk at choosing what they would like to learn about or do. You might even think that they are devoid of intrinsic motivation or that they genuinely want nothing except to receive an A. But it is important to remember that many of your students have never been given this invitation to pursue their interests, and, if they have, they have never perceived it as a genuine invitation.

As I concluded in chapter 2, the AST strategies form a Gestalt. As you become more familiar and comfortable with the process of supporting student autonomy that runs through each of the strategies, you will become more in sync with your students.

This will make it easier for you to see and feel what is going on when they are invited to pursue their interests.

HOMEWORK: IDENTIFY AN ASPECT OF THE COURSE THAT STUDENTS GET TO DETERMINE

Step 1: Identify an aspect of your course that students can be free to choose. Make sure the choice you are giving your students is a real choice. If you absolutely have to cover experimentation as a research method, then it would be a bad idea to let your students choose which research method to explore. This is because you will be compelled to pressure them into choosing the only genuine option.

Step 2: Share with your students that they are free to choose (the topic, resource, reading, activity, etc.). I have found that it is best to give the invitation along with an explanatory rationale. You might say something such as, "For this next topic, which is human development/World War I/Surrealism/boiling point, we have quite a bit of flexibility in choosing what we do. I wonder, is there anything in particular that interests you (or Do you have any unanswered questions?) about human development/ World War I/Surrealism/boiling point?"

Step 3: Be prepared with suggestions. If students are hesitating or if they cannot think of anything right away, then it can be helpful to them if you provide a few suggestions of what they might choose. I think it is best to have several different options that demonstrate the breadth of what they might choose.

Step 4: Check in with them to make sure you understand their choice. I have found that it works best when I summarize their choice back to them. For example, students once identified "trauma" as a topic for a human development course, so I prepared a worksheet with definitions, examples, and therapeutic interventions. When students seemed bored during the activity, I asked them what they had hoped they might do. They explained that they wanted to know if what they had experienced in childhood qualified as traumatic. They wanted to discuss personal experiences and be heard. When this happened, students realized that there are many different forms of trauma. Even within specific categories such as domestic physical abuse, there are a variety of forms, contexts, and consequences. We were able to see this in a real and personal way through the stories told about their own lives.

By asking them about their interests, students are given the opportunity to clarify what those interests are. When you ask questions, they further clarify. It is often clear that they lack the resources to describe their interests. It is almost as if they have never gotten to practice articulating what interests them. But, like all skills, this can be practiced and developed.

AST Strategy Three: Present Learning Activities in Need-Satisfying Ways

Presenting learning in need-satisfying ways means that topics, activities, assessments, homework, and so on are presented in a way that students' basic psychological needs are met. Those needs are competence, relatedness, and autonomy. If a student feels like their skill and ability are reflected in what they're doing, if this student is able to relate personally to other human beings during the activity, and if this student feels a significant measure of self-direction while choosing and carrying out the activity, then the kind of regulation they exhibit will trend toward the internal and intrinsic side of the regulation continuum.

By supporting students' basic psychological needs, teachers ensure that students will not feel like pawns in a game that is about funding or test scores or faculty bonuses (I am kidding about the bonuses). These students will feel like they are the players in their own game. This is unusual for organized and formal schooling, which seems to be more about militarized control than self-direction. I think that is why AST is organized around autonomy support. Perhaps also because the goal of liberal education is to produce independent thinkers and learners.

Because the other strategies emphasize autonomy support, in this section I will focus on competence support and relatedness support. The needs themselves are simple to understand and identify, but this does not mean that they are easy to support.

COMPETENCE

For my 36th birthday, my wife bought me a video game. She did so because she loves me, and because she wanted me to have an entertaining hobby that did not involve running for hours at a time. (I suspect she is making plans for the next time I am injured and cannot run.) The subject of the game is tasteless; it is also irrelevant. What is relevant is that I can play my new game on varying difficulty levels. Thinking myself a skilled sort of guy, I played it on medium difficulty and found it nearly impossible. It wasn't any fun. I was reminded at every turn how uncoordinated and ignorant I was. I wanted to mow the lawn if only to remind myself that I was not a total nincompoop.

So I changed the difficulty level to easy. Boy was it easy. I was suddenly a professional at the game. But it also wasn't any fun, because I didn't feel challenged. I longed for the uncertainty and suspense of the medium difficulty.

So it is with supporting student competence in the classroom. Instructors must find the balance between the hazards of ease and challenge. The surest way to disengage a student is to make them feel like they are children. Students are tired of feeling stupid, unskilled, inept, or incapable. Life is full of those reminders. Learning doesn't have to be one of them.

But there is also a danger at the other end: make a task too easy and your students are likely to get bored and become disengaged. Students will say, "Oh, I learned this last year!" or, "Is that all we're going to do today?" and so on.

In order to find this balance, it will be important to know where your students are coming from. With what skills are your students entering your class? How strong do they feel about these skills? What do they still feel challenged by? Table 7.1 summarizes five possible formats for conducting intake assessments, which is how you will determine students' incoming mastery of skill.

It should be observed that teachers already do versions of these five assessments throughout the school year. They are usually recognizable by the names "quiz"

Table 7.1. Assessing ability levels of entering students

Intake Assessment	Description
Survey	• A self-report survey is a mostly open-ended means of assessing student ability levels. Depending on how well the questions are designed, the results might be ambiguous. For example, students may think they know "A Lot" about your subject, but their standards and your standards do not line up. • Survey items can be open response or fixed choice. • Helpful for questions like "How many hours per week do you spend reading?" or "What is the longest paper you have written?"
Essay	• Essays or longer open-response questions provide rich artifacts for assessing writing, facility with words and ideas, critical thinking, and so on. Really any skill for which a rubric can be designed. • Assessing essays using a rubric is very time consuming.
Presentation	• A presentation can work like an essay insofar as the student presents an artifact (their presentation), which can be assessed by the instructor using a rubric. But the presentation also allows students to get to know one another, building into the assessment relatedness.
Quiz	• Quizzes are useful for asking fixed-choice questions and assessing rote knowledge about a topic.
Discussion	• Students can be asked in a group to describe their grasp of a skill or understanding of a topic. This is the simplest way with the least amount of preparation. • Students will be tempted to hide their weakness and emphasize their strengths. • Verbal acknowledgment of skill mastery does not equal skill mastery.

or "exam," and students prepare for and often receive a grade for them. But the autonomy-supportive teacher will not stop at the letter grade of the assessment; they will observe where students seem to be struggling and where they are flourishing, and will reorganize subsequent activities and expectations in a way that students will feel optimally challenged.

RELATEDNESS

The third basic psychological need is for relatedness. Being with others—listening to others, sharing with others, working alongside others, or even debating with or challenging others—increases psychological well-being.

There are many avenues that are helpful for understanding why this is the case. Biologists and anthropologists explain how humans have evolved as social animals, which means that they are more likely to flourish in groups than alone. Philosophers have explained how the words we use and the goals we have are all social constructs, which are shaped by others. Psychologists have explained how our personalities are products of primary relationships, such as the relationship to our parents.

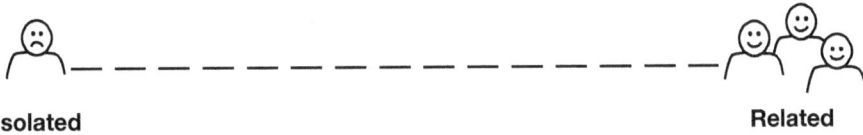

Isolated   Related

Figure 7.1.   Relation is preferable to isolation

No matter the story you prefer, the gist is the same: we do better in groups than we do by ourselves. This relationship is shown in figure 7.1.

But what about the person who prefers working alone (such as myself)? The relationship shown in figure 7.1, which is supported by books and articles and other forms of SDT research, does not mean that humans will always choose to work with others. Indeed, younger generations show greater and greater resistance to in-person socializing than generations of the past. MIT sociologist Sherry Turkle has studied this phenomenon for the past 25 years. Turkle has been particularly interested in how digital technology, which includes but is not limited to social media, has changed humans' ability to relate to one another. In her first book, Turkle (2011) describes how humans are more disconnected and isolated today than ever before. This is ironic, in her estimation, because humans are also more digitally connected to others today than ever before. But the digital connectivity does not have the same quality of being with others as one finds when sharing time and space with other living persons.

In Turkle's (2014) second book on the subject, she observes how social skills such as empathy and listening as well as self-esteem are at all-time historic lows. Teenage boys and girls, Turkle explains, now exhibit the emotional intelligence of eight year olds.

Whether or not you choose to follow Turkle's explanations, the social ineptitude she has observed is a robust phenomenon. What this means for the classroom is that there will be resistance to socializing. I have observed this even among students who are friends with one another, but it is particularly strong with students who are strangers.

I once had a quiet student confide in me after class just how proud she was that she had spoken with the student sitting next to her. She explained that she had made it her personal goal to interact more with peers, and a group-work opportunity allowed her to do so. I was particularly surprised by her comment, because I had remembered her group being the quiet one in the back. Evidently I am not always the best judge of what qualifies as relatedness.

Teachers will have to be intentional about the social component, and they will have to be gentle with how it is carried out. In order to bring about relatedness, the teacher might rely on the other two factors in promoting inner motivation: competence and autonomy. Give students something to work on together. Make sure the activity is structured and clearly explained. Be patient as they get to know and work with one another. Recognize signs of resistance, and be accepting when they occur. In other words, give students every possible chance to become social with one another, but also be willing to let them be alone. Sometimes it takes a while for shy students to emerge from their cocoon of isolation.

I once had a student who sat in quiet suspense for weeks as her classmates had lively and enthusiastic conversations all around her. I did not push or prod or coax her into participating, but showed just as much satisfaction for her timid silence as I did the earnest self-disclosure of the students sitting behind her. Then one day we were all surprised when this quiet student spoke up. It was just a comment about another student's story. I could tell that other students in class were as excited as I was that she had said something. The next class period, she said a bit more. Eventually, she was telling the most hilarious personal anecdotes that kept the entire class in stiches for minutes at a time.

At this point I am divided. Seeing this reserved young woman open up to me and others does not scream "achieving student learning outcomes." What it screams is relatedness, which isn't nearly as important to school administrations as "thinks critically" or "communicates effectively." Of course, what it also shows is that this student will be more comfortable sitting down with another human person, such as with a prospective employer during a job interview, and having a thoughtful conversation without the look and temperament of a tiny fledgling bird who has just been abandoned in the nest. I also know it means that, for this student, attending and participating in class is becoming more and more of an internally motivated decision.

PUT IT INTO PRACTICE

Homework Activity #1: Stop and Assess Where Your Students Are

For this first homework activity, it doesn't matter at what point you are within the course: Stop what you're doing and check in with your students to see how they are getting along with respect to the learning objective or objectives. This can be done by creating an open-response or closed-choice survey, it can be done in a town hall–type forum, or it can be handled by distributing slips of paper and taking handwritten responses.

Step 1: Remind students about the end goal. Take a minute to summarize the course objective(s). This has been the goal of the course all along. All of the discussions, lectures, activities, study sessions, and so on have been in service to this goal. Take a moment to reflect on the reason for it all.

It may also be helpful to ask students to reflect on what their personal goals are with respect to the objective. For example, if the objective is learning how to write a research report, then what level of mastery is each student after? When will they know that they have reached this level?

Step 2: Ask students about how they are getting along. How far along do your students feel with respect to their personal goals and the course objective(s)? Are they progressing rapidly, or do they feel like they are inching along at a glacial pace? Maybe they feel less capable now than they did when the course began.

By itself, this step will provide most of the data the teacher will need to assess whether the course is so easy that students have become disengaged or so difficult that they have become disengaged. You want to see if students feel a gentle but clear challenge.

Step 3: Ask follow-up questions to better understand what has been working and what hasn't been working. If students feel bored or helpless, then you will probably want to ask students to clarify. Clarity will help you zoom in on what the problem seems to be.

Step 4: Make changes to the course in order to keep student challenge at the optimal level.

Sample: In a methods course I was teaching, I checked in with my students before a big assessment where they would be writing the design section of their papers. It was clear from their collective malaise that they were beginning to feel helpless, but I couldn't figure out why. I confirmed that this was not in my imagination. As a follow-up, I asked them what they felt like they hadn't yet mastered. Discussion meandered for a bit as students felt out whether it would be okay to share their perceived difficulty—that they wouldn't get in trouble for admitting that they were struggling. Eventually a student explained that they still weren't sure that they understood how to state a clear hypothesis. They knew what to include in a design, but they just couldn't see its relationship to the hypothesis. They knew that this relationship was important, because their professor would not stop going on and on about it.

Looking at the course plan, I realized that I had spent fewer than 30 minutes on hypotheses. I had figured that this would have been mastered years earlier. I put the course schedule on the projection screen, and we did a little surgery. We added two weeks on hypothesis writing, which we would accommodate by lopping off one of the final sections of the course.

Homework Activity #2: Emphasize Relatedness by Encouraging Students to Work Together

Step 1: Create an opportunity for students to work together. You can ask them to work in groups or with a partner, or to collect data from (or interview) one another. Entire courses can be designed around group work, with individualized components for individualizing grades (if that is important or necessary).

Step 2: Be watchful for resistance, shyness, and interpersonal conflict. As described earlier, younger generations have greater difficulty socializing in person. They are much more skilled with digital communication. It is impossible to predict what the future holds for social relations. Perhaps one day face-to-face communication will go the way of the telegram. If you think face-to-face communication is important, then be watchful for and patient with student shyness and anxiety. If you think digital technology will be the primary medium for human communication, then design a way for your students to interact using technology.

Also remember that people do not always get along. This does not have to be prevented unless it comes to shouting or fighting or any other sort of confrontational mess. Learning that sometimes other people can be lazy, deceitful, selfish, arrogant, and so on can be a valuable bit of social learning.

PROBLEMS TO EXPECT AND HOW TO DEAL WITH THEM

Students Have a Range of Skill Levels

Ideally, students enter a course with a homogenous level of skill. No one student outperforms any other. But this is seldom how it occurs. It is likely that students will enter your course with a range of skills. Sometimes this range is enormous. Some students will already be writing in complete and error-free sentences with attention to word choice and rhythm, and others will be struggling to spell. Some students will have read or studied a good deal about the subject before entering your class, and others will only be hearing about it for the first time.

Consider a first-year writing class. If you spend two weeks on subject-verb agreement, then the students who write essays and poems in their free time will lose interest due to lack of challenge, and the student who cannot spell (let alone define) "subject" will lose interest due to the perceived level of difficulty. What can be done?

I do not have the answer for this, but I do have a few suggestions. My first suggestion is to get a feel for who the outlier is, if there is one. Are there only one or two precocious students? If so, then you might let them treat your course like an independent study where they go beyond the course learning objectives. In my college courses, I invite these gifted students to do the following:

• Help me on my research projects
• Teach a section of the course
• Lead discussions
• Create course materials (videos, quizzes, handouts)

If they have personal goals for the course that are not covered (such as goals to become a therapist), then I gather extra resources for them and meet with them privately outside of class.

I would say that about one out of three precocious students, when given the option of a more significant challenge, will take me up on it. The other two make the choice to be unchallenged, which I think is okay, too. That way they know that they are responsible for their boredom. I find that these same students take a more facilitative role in classroom discussions, which shows that they are taking on responsibility of the learning of their peers.

If, instead of one or two precocious students, you find a course with one or two students who are well behind the rest, then you can handle them in very much the same way. But you will not be pushing them further along the range of difficulty; you will be providing simpler resources and simpler objectives. The goal will be to help these students find sure footing. Once secure, they will likely be able to catch themselves up rather quickly. Their sure footing will help them feel engaged with their peers (relatedness), the material (competence), and the course objectives (autonomy).

If your course has a wide mixture of all ability levels, then bless your soul. I ordinarily have the first scenario (one or two geniuses), but here is what I might do with a potpourri of ability levels:

• Give multiple options for readings, and label them easy, medium, and hard. I recognize that this means doing three times as much preparatory work.
• Give benchmarks for assignments, with the simplest benchmark receiving an A (which is the highest possible recorded score), the medium benchmark receiving an

A+, and the hardest receiving an A++ (and so on). There is no advantage to getting an A++ except for challenging themselves.

- And so on, with all aspects of the course.

With each of these scenarios, all that is required is an adjustment of expectations. If you expect students to enter a course at, say, a level of 7 out of 10, but you find them to be at a level of 5 out of 10, then you adjust your expectations down to between 5 and 6.

Students Are Not Interested in Working Together

Whenever we make a change to our classroom, we hope that the change will be met with enthusiastic surprise. Of course this doesn't always happen. Because it is something new, students are likely to be skeptical (or even alarmed). But also because it is something new, the teacher still has some learning to do about how best to make the change.

The first time you introduce group work, you will either be relying on your idea of how it should go or the idea of somebody else, which you have read about in a book or listened to in a talk. Like all first-time experiences, you can expect that there will be a learning curve. This means that you will probably overlook some detail that seems unimportant, but that turns out to be absolutely essential. Student apathy is a good sign that there is a problem with how the groups have been organized or what students have been asked to do.

If (or when) it doesn't work out as you had imagined, then it will be helpful to lean on the other aspects of supporting student autonomy. Acknowledge and accept their nonparticipation, take the students' perspective, use explanatory rationale, and so on. Admit the possibility that you don't know the best way to organize groups for that particular class, and ask your students for their help. Explain how you understand group work to be important for developing soft skills and so on, and explain why you have organized the groups the way that you did. In other words, be completely transparent, letting your students know everything. Perhaps they misunderstood what you were asking. Perhaps they know a better way.

Provided you use each group work failure as a learning experience, each subsequent time you organize groups will benefit from the failures that came before. Soon you will be sensitive to student needs within their groups. You will begin to recognize the differences in student apathy—you will recognize when it is boredom with a topic, distraction by something in the media, or preoccupation with other coursework.

CHAPTER 8

Supporting Students' Internalization

AST Strategy Four: Provide Explanatory Rationale

When teachers design courses, or when they think through the course designs that they have been given, they do so intentionally. Resources are chosen based on their perceived relevance, importance, and attractiveness; activities are chosen based on how productive or interesting they might be; assessments are chosen or designed based on how revealing they will be. And so on. Everything has a reason behind it.

But the reason isn't always clear to the student. From my experience, at least when I dig down far enough, the reason isn't always clear to me as the instructor, either. In one particularly embarrassing and revealing personal experience, I assigned a group of general psychology students a short homework assignment over the weekend. Class discussion had run long on a Friday, and my students didn't have a chance to answer the question I hoped that they would answer, so I gave it as an open-response question to do as homework. When they came back to class the following week, I had forgotten all about the homework. "Want us to turn this in?" they asked. "Turn what in?" I asked. I realized at that moment that I had given my students homework for no other reason than to keep them occupied.

Here was my rationale for that assignment: It is important to my department chair and college dean and so on up the academic chain of command, or so it is in my imagination, that students turn in sheets of paper full of handwritten words. These sheets of paper are counted or graded or measured in some way as a representation of the rigor our students are expected to perform while enrolled at our university.

That is to say, my rationale was entirely selfish. I wanted students to complete a busywork homework assignment, because having them do so would make me feel more secure in my identity as a serious college professor.

Most college professors will not have this kind of flexibility. There may be an assigned curriculum with a common assessment at the end. Instructors might be evaluated based on how well students perform on these common assessments, and therefore the activities and course materials would have to be built upon these common end-of-course goals. If this describes your situation as you see it, then fear not:

You can still provide rationales for the resources you provide and the activities and assessments you conduct.

A rationale is the reasoning behind a given resource or activity. For example: "Why do we have to read—why can't we just watch a video?" Because reading is an active process where the reader has to make hundreds of decisions about the meanings of marks on the page. Watching a YouTube video is a passive consumption of information. While both are means of consuming information, reading sharpens thinking, decision making, problem solving, creativity, and so on. It is the superior method of learning.

When students (or workers or loved ones) are given the rationale behind something, then they are less likely to feel as though they have been blindfolded. They are more likely to give themselves over to an activity when they understand its significance. In a previous example where students volunteered to write weekly essays for no other reason than that it would make me look better as their instructor, this was because they understood why it was important, even though it didn't directly concern them. They had all of the information, which they could weigh while making their decision. They weren't prepared to write from some unknown and mysterious reason; they were writing to help support the self-esteem and self-concept of their anxious instructor.

It is more common that students are kept in the dark about the work they are doing. Students are told to work hard for reasons that cannot be explained. They are told about how, "One day you'll be happy that you did!" and, "Because it is important!" and, "Because I told you so!"

PUT IT INTO PRACTICE

Homework Activity #1: Explain Why You're Doing the Next Thing You Will Be Doing

It doesn't matter what the next thing is: explain why it cannot be omitted from your course. If you cannot explain this to yourself, then rethink why it is included at all.

If you begin class by taking attendance, then explain why that is important. For example: "For legal reasons, the university requires that I take a daily log of students' whereabouts," or, "College policy states that students cannot have more than three absences per course," or "Reading your names aloud and then pairing those names with your faces is how I learn your names."

If you plan on giving a 50-minute lecture, then explain why it is important to do so in person, and why an oral lecture is more valuable than time spent reading, writing, or talking about a subject.

Step 1: Identify the next thing you will be doing for a course. This can be as easy as walking into the classroom and asking yourself, "What is the first thing that I will be doing with students?"

Step 2: Explain why that next thing is important. Free associate. Speak freely. This doesn't have to be a logical proof. Just explain, to the best of your ability, why the lecture or handout or reading is important.

You might not have any reason prepared. In this case, you may wish to brainstorm ahead of time: "Why *do* I lecture these points?" or, "Why *do* I require that students wear nametags?" or, "Why *do* I ask students to complete these handouts?"

If your reasoning is unsatisfying to you, then it will probably also be unsatisfying to your students. Take some time to think about alternatives. If you feel comfortable doing so, then let your students participate in this process.

Homework Activity #2: Integrate Rationale into Assignment Instructions

Step 1: Find an assignment. Go through your personal catalog of activities and assignments and pick one that you will be using in the near future.

Step 2: Add to the instructions your rationale for the assignment. In the section where you tell students what they need to do in order to complete the assignment, provide a short statement where you include the following:

a. Why the assignment is important
b. How the assignment will facilitate item a.

If this seems awkward at first, then it means that there is room for growth in how autonomy supportive you can be with your students. This is a good thing. The more you do it, the easier it will be. This will provide a sort of self-assessment of how you are changing as an instructor.

Step 3 (optional): Get student feedback. When students read the rationale, do they understand what you're saying? Do they share your perspective about what is important? After they complete the assignment, do they feel like it facilitated what you hoped it would facilitate? Take whatever feedback your students give and use it to change the assignments (or even the course objectives).

Homework Activity #3: Explore the TiLT Model of Teaching

Workshop attendees have claimed, and I have confirmed, that step 3 of supporting student autonomy is very similar to an exciting "new" method that is sweeping through K–12 and higher education. It is called TiLT, which stands for "transparency in learning and teaching." You can read more about it in a new book by Akella et al. (2022).

AST Strategy Five: Acknowledge Negative Feelings

It is interesting to me that AST scholars specify that teachers are to accept negative affect. I wanted to ask, "Does that mean I can turn a blind eye to positive affect?" Of course, the answer is "no." I realized that as soon as I asked the question. No instructor has trouble accepting or sympathizing with a student who is happy, eager, or confident, because these positive emotions will make the teacher feel these ways, too. Emotions are infectious.

Students, just like instructors, are whole persons. This means that they are more than their intellects. They are bodies, too, which come with lots of complicated organ systems such as the hypothalamic, pituitary, and adrenal systems. Despite taking millions of years to evolve in complexity, this organic tissue regularly impedes thinking, reasoning, and problem solving.

Students, just like their instructors, also have rich lives outside of the classroom. They have relationships, aspirations, and challenges that are sometimes completely unrelated to institutionalized learning. These parts of students' personalities are still present even though the instructors do not have access to them; and they are still important even though instructors might not understand why.

In order to accept these unseen depths and breadths of students, an instructor is advised to accept their students completely. This happens naturally with positive emotions but requires a bit of diligence with negative emotions. This, I believe, is the rationale behind AST strategy number five.

Homework Activity #1: Acknowledge and Accept the Negative Affect of One Student

Step 1: Notice and name the negative affect. The next time you are in the classroom (or in your office reading emails from students), identify the negative affect of at least one student. Name the affect (in your head; you needn't call the student out). You might say to yourself, "I see that you are frustrated," or "I can see that you are upset," or "I notice that you are nervous."

Step 2: Accept the negative affect. This is the tricky part: the goal is not to transform the negative affect into something positive. Even if the student appears to be languishing in misery, the purpose of acknowledging and accepting negative affect is to let that student continue to be as they are.

Step 3: Don't take it any further. This is a second reminder not to try and change the negative affect you have identified. You may be tempted to adjust an assignment or activity in order to placate the student or to take it easy on them. But this isn't a game. Your students are not trying to manipulate you, nor are you trying to manipulate them. Sometimes people are upset. Being upset can make work more difficult. This is okay.

By accepting the negative emotion you are telling the student and anybody who is watching that the classroom is a place for students, no matter how happy, inspired, or deferential those students are.

Homework Activity #2: Use Collective Negative Affect as a Diagnostic Tool

Step 1: Notice the next time the majority of students are disengaged, tired, apathetic, or are exhibiting some other form of negative affect. Perhaps you have just asked a question or introduced an activity, but nobody is doing anything. You were hoping that students would answer the question creatively or would begin the activity enthusiastically, but instead their eyes are half-closed, they're staring at their phones, or they're chit-chatting with each other. In other words, you find yourself in a teaching nightmare kind of situation.

Rather than become defensive or domineering, treat your observations as data that tell you that your plans for class that day are not as good as you thought they were.

Even without trying, students are giving you helpful feedback. Their feedback is as follows: "We don't much like what you have planned for the day."

Step 2: Acknowledge this negative affect without pointing fingers. It will be very difficult to avoid becoming authoritarian. Criticisms of laziness, irresponsibility, and immaturity will dance across your consciousness. Refrain from following them.

Instead, accept that maybe the plan for the day could be better, and that students are doing everything in their limited repertoire of student behaviors to communicate this understanding. Of course it would be wonderful if they could use their words, but it is unusual that students are allowed to say things that begin with "I don't like it when you, the teacher, . . ."

Step 3: Give suggestions about what the class might do instead. Following the advice of Reeve (2016), it will be helpful to your students if you gave sample alternatives to the classroom activity that failed to capture your students' attention. Come up with two or three reasonable alternatives from which students can choose. They don't all have to be "watch a video on YouTube," either. By giving options, you are vitalizing your students' inner motivational resources (specifically autonomy).

Step 4: Seek feedback on engaging activities. You might find that the alternatives you suggest are about as interesting as different flavors of vanilla ice cream. In that event, you may pull a page from AST step 1 ("Take Students' Perspective") and consult your students directly about how to best handle chronic apathy.

Sample: Whenever classes resume after mid-term holiday, the foot scuffing of students (and sometimes their faculty) is noticeably pronounced. In my experience, it usually takes a few days before engagement and interest return to the classroom discussions and activities.

After one spring break, I had trouble overcoming the inertia of sitting on my own couch. When I made it to the classroom, I noticed the same kind of apathy in my students. I considered the lesson plan I had for the day, which was a continuation of a topic we had begun two weeks before. I could sense that it would wind up being a lot of me talking and students trying not to fall asleep. I decided to emphasize one of the other course objectives instead, which was about trying to get to know my students better (and encouraging them to get to know each other better). This led to a lively discussion about vacations, college life, what comes next, and so on. With 20 minutes left, my students apologized and asked if there was something that I wanted them to do. I explained that I was very pleased with what had already happened, and that I wondered if anybody had wanted to continue our conversation from before break. We actually stayed a little bit after class time had ended in discussion.

I must admit that it doesn't always go so well. Sometimes, as I have already shared, I am way off the mark when it comes to acknowledging students' negative affect. But each time I have misunderstood, I use that as a learning experience so that I am not so far off the next time. And the next time.

Homework Activity #3: Reflect on the Ideal Emotional Profile of Students

(Note: When I drafted this, I thought that reflecting on my own hopes for student affect would be useful for accepting when a student does not behave like the students in my fantasy. However, I realized that this ended up being less about accepting negative affect and more about identifying my own goals and expectations for teaching and learning. I have decided to keep it, because it shows the interconnection between the seven steps for supporting student autonomy. Take from this exercise what you will.)

In order to recognize negative emotions in students, I think it is helpful to reflect on your hopes and expectations for how you think students ought to be feeling in your class. This isn't the time to pretend like you are an endless fountain of empathy and concern. Imagine the temperament and interest level of your perfect student or your perfect classroom. Be creative. Get fantastical. What sorts of observations would they have about you? What would they be interested in?

Here is what it looks like for me: All of my students attend on my imaginary perfect day. They show up before class begins, and sit in quiet anticipation a full minute before class starts. One student apologizes before asking a question about the topic for the day. You see, this imaginary perfect student has read everything that they could find about the topic, including something obscure that I had published years earlier, and they have already gone through the trouble of synthesizing it. In other words, class time is spent in discussion with younger and differently opinioned versions of myself.

By writing my wildest fantasy about how a class period will go, I can see that genuine passion and interest are important to me. If I am interested in promoting genuine passion, then that means I will probably have to adjust my learning objectives for class. Instead of "thinking critically about $x, y,$ and $z,$" which requires learning about x through z and then applying what was learned and so on, I would have to let students explore what genuinely interests them about x through $z,$ and then help them do so.

Step 1: Write your fantasy. On a piece of paper (or blank document), write out your fantasy for how students behave and feel and interact with each other during class.

Step 2: Acknowledge that your fantasy is in your imagination. Recognize how your fantasy is make believe.

Step 3: Identify what seems to be most important to you. What does your fantasy tell you about what you want students to be doing? How might you reengineer your course in order to bring about the learning objectives that seem closer to your goals?

AST Strategy Six: Rely on Invitational Language

While giving a workshop on AST as part of a larger teaching conference, my colleague Liz Kuipers and I had participants work together in groups to design a way to apply AST in an online course. One of the groups was really struggling with how to use informational, nonpressuring language.

"They can either do the assignment," said one participant, "or they can choose *not* to do the assignment." It was clear from their wry smile that this teacher didn't really think that this "invitational" approach would be terribly helpful. And, of course, she was right. Choosing between passing and failing isn't really a choice.

In order to understand and appreciate the sixth AST strategy, it helps to reexamine what it means to promote student autonomy. With autonomy, a learner's regulation of behaviors becomes internalized. This means that they begin to adopt learning activities as their own. If the student really doesn't have a choice in the matter, then it would be a bad time to invite them to make a choice. In those cases, explanatory rationale might be more helpful.

Now consider an aspect of the course that is not rigidly defined, such as how a given learning objective is achieved. Say, for example, the objective is to develop effective written communication skills. There are hundreds of activities that could promote this learning objective, such as free writing, formal writing, writing essays or poems or screen plays, reading, summarizing, keeping a journal, and so on. An instructor may prefer journal writing, and will invite their students to keep a regular journal. But this instructor also realizes that there are many activities that will help students develop their writing skills, and will therefore be open to alternatives that students might prefer.

For example, an instructor may use invitational language in the following way:

> Part of communicating effectively through written word is the skill of concision, which means saying something in the fewest possible words. This is difficult, because every writing teacher you have had since the third grade has used word count as the primary target of writing activities, which teaches you to say things in as many words as possible. To combat this tendency for a writer to go on and on and on about nothing in particular, I have found it helpful to write Haikus. A Haiku is a poem limited to 17 syllables. This might only be 10 or 11 words, which is much shorter than a 1,500-word essay. But it is very difficult to say something meaningful using so few syllables.
>
> For this activity, I would like you to try your hand at writing a Haiku. Do this by thinking of something you want to say, then figuring out a way to say it in exactly 17 syllables.

In this example activity, I have introduced it by describing its significance, its purpose, and its steps. At no point is a demand made or threat given.

At the moment, I cannot imagine a better activity for practicing concision. But this doesn't mean that a student will not have a better idea. If a student asks if they could write a limerick instead, or if they want to summarize *Gone with the Wind* using 25 syllables, then I cannot imagine a teacher who would scowl in disapproval.

In some cases the activity might be fixed. Certificate and licensure programs often have fixed requirements, such as clinical supervisions for nursing students or lesson plan development for teachers in training. In these cases, the instructor will want to make it clear to their students that the requirements are set by regional accrediting bodies, and that they are necessary if the goal is obtaining the certificate or license. Still, this can be said in a pressuring way or in a nonpressuring way.

Pressuring way: You have to write a lesson plan, or else you will fail this course.

Nonpressuring way: If your goal is to one day obtain your teaching license, then part of that is being able to write a lesson plan.

It may come as a surprise, but students sometimes enroll in certification programs with no interest in becoming certified. I just met with a social work professor who couldn't believe that her student—a football player—was going to enroll in a master of social work program in order to get his final year of eligibility. He had no interest in becoming a social worker, at least not at the time. He was only interested in his eligibility. For this student, the situation can be expressed as follows:

Pressuring way: You have to write a case plan, or else you will fail.

Nonpressuring way: If you want to get your final year of eligibility, then that means that you will have to be admitted to the graduate program. Unfortunately, not everybody who applies is admitted. In particular, we are looking for students who have not only passed their undergraduate courses, but who have excelled at the clinical skills (such as writing case reports).

Homework Activity #1: Rewrite Activity Instructions Using Invitational Language

For this homework, it doesn't matter which component of class you choose; you will rewrite the instructions for it (even if it is something for which you don't ordinarily give instructions). For example, if you plan on giving a lecture, taking attendance, or asking students to free write for the first ten minutes of class, then write the instructions for what they will be doing using informational, nonpressuring language.

Step 1: Choose the activity.

Step 2: Write instructions using invitational language. The more unusual it seems to do this, the more helpful it will be. When is the last time you gave instructions for a lecture?

"World War I history is very complex, and students often get confused when reading information about it. So I have summarized what seem to me to be the most important and interesting parts of this period. I have organized this summary around bullet points and photographs, which I will share via the projector screen. You might choose to sit and listen, take notes, ask questions, or check your email until I have finished."

Step 3: Reflect on your instructions. Are you satisfied with the activity as you have described it? Has the description caused you to rethink any parts of the activity or to make any changes? Does the activity seem more/less important?

Homework Activity #2: Design an Alternative Assignment

For this homework, choose an assignment that has become a staple for one of your courses. Maybe it is a test, quiz, or essay. Don't worry, you will not have to make any changes to the assignment or to your course.

Step 1: Choose an assignment. Try to pick one that you have come to rely on.

Step 2: Write the instructions using informational, nonpressuring language. Follow the steps in the first homework activity.

Step 3: Using the same rationale, design a new assignment that accomplishes the same objective. Do this even if the new assignment doesn't seem like it would be as good as your personal favorite.

You might do this step with a student who excels at creative thinking.

Step 4 (optional): Get students' perspective of the new assignment. Ask a volunteer to complete the new assignment, and get their feedback (AST workshop 1).

AST Strategy Seven: Practice Patience

If you have made it through the other six AST strategies, then you have already practiced patience many times. By taking time to consider your students' point of view, for example, you are already more sensitive and attentive to how they are getting along. You will notice when they are following along, when they are struggling to keep focus, or when they have lost interest. You are more in tune (or more in sync) with your students.

In order to be patient with a student (or anyone, really), you have to recognize that people work in different ways and at different speeds. Some students read quickly. Some students need a lot of examples. Some students can turn objects around in their minds with ease and facility. Practicing patience means letting each of these students be students in their own unique ways.

Homework Activity #1: Adjust the Amount of Time Needed for Completing an Activity

Say that your course schedule calls for students to complete a handout or journal entry. Rather than using a round but otherwise arbitrary measure of time, such as 10 or 15 minutes, let your students work until they are satisfied with the activity.

Step 1: Identify the activity. It doesn't matter what the activity is. It can be a lecture or video or quiz. Just choose the next thing you plan on doing for your class.

Step 2: Be prepared to adjust the amount of time necessary for the activity. You might plan on covering five concepts during a 35-minute lecture. That is fine. But this step asks you to be prepared to make changes, provided those changes seem necessary. Ask yourself: "After covering concept number one, do students seem to be following along?" "Have they lost interest?" "Have *I* lost interest?" And so on.

Step 3: Make the necessary adjustment. If students are struggling to understand the first concept, then maybe provide another example. Then another. In order to help them really master it before moving onto concept number two, maybe have them put it to use by giving an example or explaining it in their own words.

You might find that the entire class period was spent covering the one concept, but that by doing so your students were able to follow along. They felt optimally challenged and therefore engaged, they (and you) felt satisfied, and other marvelous things occurred. You might even decide to adjust the entire course schedule to allow for a more patient development of thinking and learning about the course materials and objectives.

For example, when I first started teaching college students, I imagined that they would arrive with a basic understanding of psychology. I believed that they already knew what the general consensus was among psychologists about personality or how learning occurs. I was committing a cognitive fallacy that is common in toddlers: I was being egocentric.

Egocentrism does not only mean that a person believes that the world revolves around them. For toddlers, egocentrism means that the toddler's understanding is shared by everybody else. If a toddler thinks that a television show is boring, then *everybody* must think that the television show is boring. Like the toddler, I had mistaken my understanding of psychology for the understanding that an ordinary college student would have. Because of this misunderstanding, I was struggling to figure out why, for example, my students were so confused by the existential-phenomenological critique of contemporary psychopathology.

After years and years of practice, and learning how to adjust my expectations, I am beginning to be more patient with my students. Instead of taking for granted that they know about the psychosocial moratorium (where young people try out many personalities) and its creator (Erik Erikson), I first take time to introduce them to the familiar problem of finding themselves. And so on. We move much more slowly.

By the time you are reading this, I will probably be moving more slowly still. This is not to say that my students continue to disappoint me. It means that I am still learning how to think and learn alongside my students, and that I am still learning that more is not always better.

Homework Activity #2: Patient Listening

Patience can be practiced during a conversation or classroom discussion. This is the simplest homework activity across each of the workshops, because it only takes around five seconds. But simple and quick doesn't mean that it will be easy.

I have noticed that there is an enormous difference between the perception of time as a speaker and the perception of time as a member of the audience. This change happened somewhere around graduate school, when a 20-minute presentation went from being a lot of time to fill to becoming barely enough time to introduce a topic. After teaching 60-minute and 90-minute and three-hour courses, an hour no longer seems like a lot of time. To compensate, I found that I had developed the habit of rushing classroom discussions along as quickly as possible—often steering them in the direction I thought they needed to go.

If this sounds like something you have done or are currently doing, then this will be an uncomfortable but helpful activity.

It is eminently simple: the next time you ask a question or invite students to share their input, wait the amount of time you ordinarily wait before speaking, and then wait a bit longer. Count to five or 10 in your head before jumping in with what you want to say.

Step 1: Ask your students a question or invite them to share. If they don't start answering or sharing right way, then:

Step 2: Wait the amount of time that you ordinarily wait for them to speak. If they still haven't started answering or sharing, then:

Step 3: Count to five or 10 or 20. The silence and inactivity will be almost impossible to bear. But count to five or 10 or 20 anyway. Don't count so fast that the consonants mesh together, either. None of that "onetwothreefourfivesixeveneight-nine." Count slowly.

Once you become comfortable with 10 seconds and 20 seconds, you might find your comfort growing with entire minutes of empty space. As you become more comfortable with being silent, your students will become more comfortable being the ones who are doing the talking. In my experience, the first few times it may take a long pause before students will begin talking. This is because, over the years, they have learned that it is the teachers who do all the questioning, answering, sharing, and so on. All the students have to do is bite their tongues for 10 seconds, and the teacher will give up. That's how it usually works. So, the first time, they wait for an uncomfortably long period before answering the question.

But be prepared. Their answer will be some version of "Can you repeat the question?" Try not to be upset by this. Their question shows an important shift in their perception. The first time you asked your question, your students were not really paying attention. Why should they? Teachers never give them enough time to respond thoughtfully anyhow. But the second time you ask it, your students will be listening. They will be actively involved in what you're saying.

In subsequent exchanges, the amount of time you have to wait will be less and less. It will also become less and less common for students to ignore you the first time around. Eventually, the students themselves will be asking one another thoughtful questions—questions that you hadn't even thought of on your better days.

Part III

FINISHING TOUCHES

CHAPTER 9

Sample Assessment of Using Autonomy Support in an Online Course

The evidence in favor of autonomy-supportive teaching is substantial. It tells us that if teachers can create conditions where students feel that their autonomy is supported, then those students will internalize their learning more deeply. Internalized regulation facilitates learning that is natural, satisfying, and long lasting.

But just because a teacher has the intention of supporting student autonomy doesn't mean that they will be effective at doing so. Misunderstandings about how to acknowledge and accept negative affect or uncertainty about how to provide structure may inhibit the autonomy-supportive environment that is desired. Therefore a teacher might be interested in testing to see whether or not the changes they have made to the classroom environment and structure of their courses have had the outcomes they were hoping for. This chapter provides a sample of this process as it unfolded in a pair of online courses I taught during a summer semester.

In chapter 5, I differentiated assessment from evaluation. I explained how assessment is a continually evolving process of self-improvement, and it might include a wide variety of data sources. The question at the root of assessment is, "How can I be doing a better job?" Evaluation, by comparison, is a test of the effectiveness of something, which, in this case, is a new teaching strategy. The question at the root of evaluation is, "Does the strategy do what I wanted it to do?" or, more simply, "Does it work?"

In this chapter, I share examples of each. I evaluate the effectiveness of my autonomy-supportive teaching intervention by collecting outcome data and doing a mean comparison with a control group. For the assessment, I analyzed my own reflections, student feedback, student artifacts, and any other events that stood out to me as significant. I found the assessment to be significantly more interesting and informative than the evaluation.

AST in Online Courses: An Understudied Relationship

One of my reasons for studying the effectiveness of AST in my online courses was that there is very little support for it in the literature. Despite a wealth of research support for AST in traditional face-to-face courses, the verdict is still out on whether AST is useful as a teaching strategy in online courses.

As late as 2019, Wang and others have observed how AST "is one of the most comprehensive and empirically supported motivation theories in educational settings, [. . .] but not in the online learning environment" (Wang et al., 2019, pp. 114–115).

Maybe this is because few studies have been conducted on the relationship between autonomy support and learning in online classrooms. A notable exception is a study by Chen and Jang (2010), who tested a model for online learner motivation on a group of 262 students completing online certificate programs. What they found, however, was that self-determination measures failed to predict learning outcomes. This means that learning conditions that improved perceived autonomy support did not increase student achievement. In other words, AST didn't seem to work in online courses.

In the more recent example, Wang and others focused on why AST works in face-to-face courses, yet fails to work in online courses. They wondered whether or not online students had different preferences for autonomy support, so they tested the validity of the autonomy support inventories with online students. These inventories, you will recall, examine the components of self-determined behavior and include competence, relatedness, autonomy, need satisfaction, and need dissatisfaction.

In ordinary face-to-face courses, supporting student competence, relatedness, and autonomy leads to an increase in need satisfaction. Or, if student autonomy or competence are thwarted, then this increases need dissatisfaction. But when these five factors were tested in the online environment, a few of the measures of relatedness and autonomy did not correlate with need dis/satisfaction as anticipated. This meant that students had different expectations for, and they felt differently about, relatedness and autonomy when taking online courses as compared to taking face-to-face courses.

One of the relatedness items that did not correlate with need dissatisfaction as expected was the statement, "I pretty much keep to myself when in this course," which, as an example of social isolation, was expected to lead to need dissatisfaction. With online students, however, *this is not perceived as a problem*. The second relatedness item, which also didn't seem to bother students, was, "There are not many people in this course that I am close to" (Wang et al., 2019, p. 117).

The autonomy item that is generally perceived as an issue in ordinary face-to-face courses, but which didn't seem to bother online students, was the statement, "When I am in this course, I have to do what I am told." Online students don't seem to mind it when teachers gave clear though inflexible requirements.

If we take these items together, then we can say that online students have adjusted their expectations when it comes to relating with others and exercising autonomy. More specifically, students in online courses have lowered their expectations for relatedness, possibly because they are not sharing space and time with others and therefore do not perceive it as a deficit or as need dissatisfying to participate in an asynchronous class in a low-interaction environment.

When these three specific items were dropped, there was a stronger relationship between self-determination factors and learning outcomes. When those three items were discarded, perceived autonomy support was predictive of the students' learning objective achievement and need satisfaction in online courses.

With some evidence that autonomy-supportive teaching can improve student achievement and boost their self-determination in online courses, I designed a strategy to test this relationship myself.

Design

To evaluate the effectiveness of my AST strategies I used a matched groups comparison with nonrandom assignment. More specifically, I compared two of my courses (in which I used AST strategies) with two courses taught by a colleague of mine who was willing to distribute the learning climate inventory (Williams et al., 1994) to his students.

All courses were similar in a variety of ways. All were listed as courses in the social sciences. They were courses listed at the first- and second-year level. And they were 100% asynchronous. My colleague and I are alike in our desire to be good instructors, and we have been teaching at our university for the same amount of time. The main difference between my courses and his was that I had organized my courses around the AST strategies, and my colleague had not.

Both sets of courses provided students with a learning climate inventory, which had been built into the online classroom as a quiz. In the control condition, the inventory was a requirement. In the AST condition, the inventory was optional.

CONTROL CONDITION

My colleague was asked to teach his courses the way he would ordinarily. For him, this meant four discussion posts and four exams. Because this colleague is interested in providing a warm and sympathetic environment for his students, he was very quick to respond to student emails, solve problems, give suggestions, troubleshoot, and so on. He has also developed his coursework with attention to student interests, current events, and social evolution. In other words, the instructor in the control condition was already quite a bit more autonomy supportive than, say, a joyless and stiff-lipped drill sergeant kind of instructor.

AST CONDITION

Students enrolled in the AST condition courses (PSYC 101, PSYC 203) found one additional learning outcome in their syllabus. This learning outcome was AST-specific, and read as follows: "Students will view themselves as the primary agents of change in their lives (i.e., their autonomy will be strengthened)."

The eight-week summer semester was broken into quarters, each two weeks long. The instructions for students were as follows:

> For each quarter, you may choose any assignments or activities that you think would substantially contribute to your learning and personal development. A

Table 9.1. Course schedule for AST condition

Activity and/or Description		
Assignments		Grade
Quarter 1	Assorted activities	100 points
Quarter 2	Assorted activities	100 points
Quarter 3	Assorted activities	100 points
Quarter 4	Assorted activities	100 points

list of assignments/activities is below, along with the number of points you can receive for completion in a satisfactory way (satisfactory = significantly contributes to your learning). The maximum number of points you can earn per quarter is 100.

Students in the AST courses were given the following list of activities to choose between, along with sample point totals. Complete activity descriptions were provided as files in the online course, along with examples.

List of Sample Activities for AST Condition (Human Growth and Development)

- Research   10–50 points
- Take an exam   50 points
- Naturalistic observation   10–50 points
- Interview a relative   10–50 points
- Complete and document a self-improvement activity   10–50 points
- Read/watch and create   10–20 points
- Complete a personal inventory   10 points
- Administer a test for a disability   10 points
- Write an essay   10 points
- Call the professor   10 points
- Demonstrate a psychological concept   10 points

Students were also given the following two examples, which students might follow.

For example, if a student wanted to get an A, then they might do the following:

Quarter One: (In this example, the student is particularly interested in child development)

- Called the professor to get clarity about what is expected this semester. **10 points**
- 10-hour observation: Observed a toddler (nephew of mine) for 10 hours over the weekend, kept a journal, and completed the observation reflection. **50 points**
- Watched a TED talk about development over the first three years (https://www.youtube.com/watch?v=K1slVo3BNtM), and wrote an essay explaining how it applied to the nephew observed. **10 points**
- Administered the ADHD test on my niece, and completed the test-administration reflection. **10 points**

- Completed two personal inventories (and inventory reflections):
  - Locus of control. **10 points**
  - Occupational interest survey. **10 points**
- **TOTAL: 100 points (A+)**

  OR

  Quarter One: (In this example, the student is particularly interested in late adulthood)

- Could not call professor. Instead, sent sample outline of activities to professor for feedback. We corresponded by email. **10 points**
- Two-hour observation: I visited my grandmother in a retirement home over the weekend and completed the observation reflection. **10 points**
- Administered an Alzheimer's test on my grandmother and completed the reflection. **10 points**
- Interviewed an assisted living supervisor and asked a series of questions I had prepared about a career in that field. **20 points**
- I watched three videos on grief counseling, and made a YouTube video where I gave advice to people mourning the loss of a loved one. **30 points**
  - Videos I watched:
  - Video 1:
  - Video 2:
  - Video 3:
  - My YouTube video:
- I talked about grief with my neighbor whose husband passed away, and completed the interview reflection. **10 points**
- **TOTAL: 90 points (A)**

Students in the AST condition submitted a set of activities each quarter of the semester, assigning whichever point values to assignments they felt they had earned. The semester was front loaded with meetings with the professor to get clarity about expectations.

Results

LEARNING CLIMATE INVENTORY

Perceived autonomy support was gathered in both conditions using the learning climate inventory (Williams et al., 1994). Student responses indicated high levels of perceived autonomy support in both conditions (which is a good problem to have). Means were compared between conditions, and the difference was small but statistically insignificant. The figures are listed in table 9.2.

The data from the learning climate inventory were inconclusive. I cannot claim that my efforts to allow for choice increased their perception of autonomy support over a course with greater control over requirements.

Table 9.2.   Mean comparison of perceived autonomy support in control and AST conditions

	Sample Size	Perceived Autonomy Support (Average) Out of 100	Standard Deviation
Control	34	91	9.2
AST	45	92	7.1

Note: $p < 0.5$.

Discussion

After conducting the mean comparison, I have concluded that four factors contributed to the inconclusive data set.

The first factor was introduced in the introduction. Wang and colleagues had observed that students in online courses are less likely to perceive controlling language as need dissatisfying. Therefore it is not surprising that there didn't seem to be a significant difference between an online course where students were told what to do versus one where they had wide liberty to choose activities on their own.

Second, and anecdotally, my colleague and I agreed that students in summer courses have a much higher activity completion rate than do students in fall or spring courses. This means that they are, by and large, more sympathetic to what their instructors are asking them to do. This would have resulted in a bias for high levels of perceived autonomy support.

Third, the sample sizes were too small for a reliable sample (34 students in the control condition, and 40 in the AST condition).

Fourth, I suspect that the changes made for the purposes of supporting student autonomy in the AST condition were not substantial enough. After studying the instructional strategies for another year and developing skills for achieving them in the classroom, I have concluded that the changes made for the summer 2021 courses were negligible. This would have limited the degree to which students would notice the impact of autonomy support.

Additional Results

Additional data were gathered for the purposes of comparing the control condition with the AST condition. These include descriptive data about course activities and student feedback. Students in the AST condition completed nearly twice as many activities as did students in the control condition. Students in the AST condition also showed high levels of creativity and curiosity in the activities they chose, whereas students in the control condition were limited to the required discussion posts and exams.

In order to correct for the disparity in sample sizes between control and AST conditions, the results of each have been corrected to reflect a sample size of 40. For example, all students in the control sample completed four exams (34 students × 4 exams = 136 exams). This total number has been modified to represent a sample size of 40 [(136 / 34) × 40 = 160].

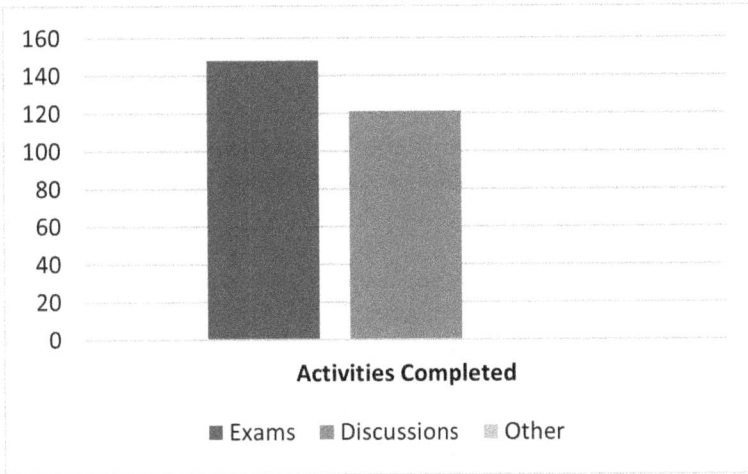

Figure 9.1. Total activities completed by students in control condition

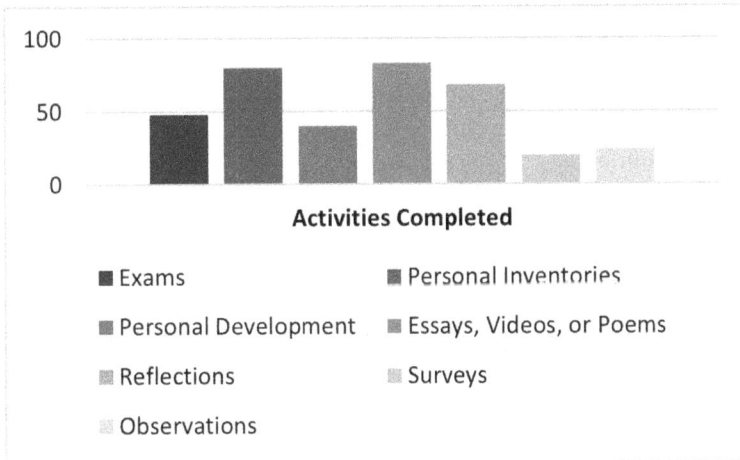

Figure 9.2. Total activities completed by students in AST condition

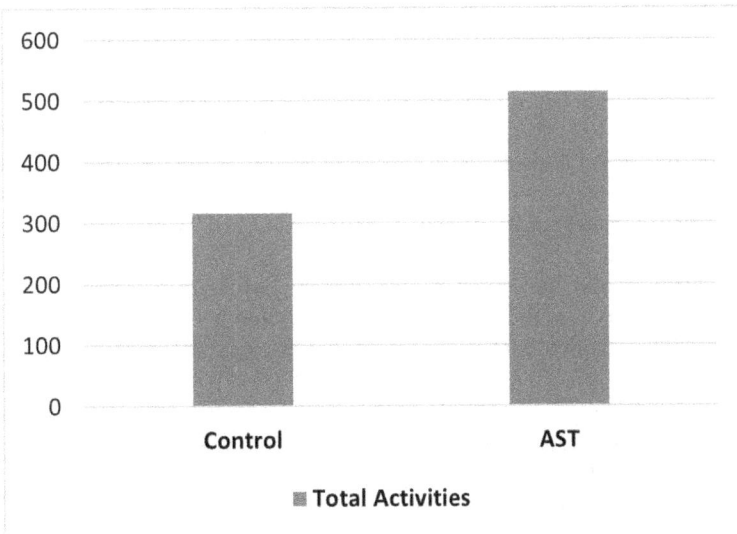

Figure 9.3. Comparison of activities completed between control and AST conditions

The majority of the students in the control courses completed the required assignments, but nothing else. This included four examinations and four discussion posts.

Students in the AST condition also had the option of completing four exams and four discussion posts, which would have amounted to the same number of points. As is shown in the graph in figure 9.2, only about one-third of exams were taken. Students organized their own requirements by choosing from a variety of alternative activities. Something that the graph does not show is how students often overreached on their point totals. That is to say, if 100 points of activities was the ceiling of what they could earn during each two-week quarter, many students completed enough activities to earn up to 160 points per quarter. One student completed 260 points for a quarter.

By itself, the significant difference in total activities completed and variety of activities completed, however interesting, is an insignificant finding. If an objective of the course is to promote creativity, then this finding might be significant. As it stands, the difference in total activities completed simply demonstrates that students in the AST condition completed activities that earned them fewer points, and therefore required a greater number.

It is also worth mentioning that students in both conditions had an equal likelihood of completing the learning climate inventory, even though it was only required in the control condition.

Student Comments about the AST Condition

Students in the AST courses were invited to share any feedback that they had about the course. About half of the students did so. The following are samples of what those students had to say:

> In the beginning of the semester I thought I wouldn't like the class because I felt it lacked structure. I like to know what I need to do and how it's to be done. This class was nothing like that! I found myself wondering what to do, which activities I would choose from, and if I would even have time to complete them all. However once I figured out what I wanted to do the ball started rolling. The structure I thought the class lacked in the beginning was the structure I then created for myself because this class forces you to do so. Often times we don't recognize our strengths [because we] magnify our weaknesses. I learned so much about myself, achieved a few milestones, and set new goals. I found the independent structure of the class to be most beneficial because it made me more autonomous. Overall I enjoyed the class although I didn't think I would in the beginning. I found you to be most encouraging, and appreciated the feedback. I think every student should experience a class with independent structure cause it is a great learning experience. Thank you for pushing me out of my comfort zone!!

> I'm learning quite a bit although my overall grade may not reflect that fact. The coursework has caused me to do a lot of valuable introspection as it relates to some of the concepts and theories and I sort of validate the information that I'm learning by applying it to my own personal experience.

It's a pleasure being your student. Thank you for sharing your insights and knowledge, guiding me, and giving me an opportunity to grow beyond the coursework. I've never been in a class like this before.

Over the past eight weeks, I have really grown to enjoy your class. This class has been one of my favorite classes I have ever taken at Albany State University. One thing that I liked about your class is how you let us pick what we want to do. I like this because it helps us improve the way we learn and gives us responsibility for our actions. Another thing that I like about your class is how I am able to learn many things and not feel pressured to do it one way but can find many ways to do it. In conclusion, I have nothing negative to say about your class and hope you have a wonderful rest of your summer.

To say that I have enjoyed this course is an understatement. I developed a lot of new knowledge through it. Not only have I learned new concepts, I have also been able to make new correlations between physiology and psychology and corrected some misconceptions. Although I believe that I would have benefited more from meeting with you in the classroom, I certainly felt supported through email and also through the structure of the online course. I reported that I felt intimidated and nearly incompetent at the beginning of the semester. Drinking from a fire hose seems like a good metaphor for my experience, but now I'm certainly more confident and competent now. Thank you for everything.

This course gave us the opportunity to be creative and I was able to learn a lot about myself in this course. Since I got to Albany you have been the most engaged professor I've had who actually cares about their student's lives and what is going on and giving honest feedback on each of our assignments. Each quarter I felt motivated to accomplish something new so thank you for an amazing summer.

Hi Professor Whitehead! I can honestly say I have enjoyed taking your class, Human Growth and Development. Between working full time, taking another class (lab course), and taking care of everything in my personal life, I have stayed super busy and sacrificed a lot of sleep over the past eight weeks. I have found myself sometimes struggling to keep up with everything. But I am very grateful that this class gave me the flexibility to choose what I wanted to learn and write about and had very reasonable deadlines. I think more classes should be designed this way, especially since so many college students are older adults with busy lives outside of school. Real life can be hectic, but it shouldn't prevent someone from furthering their education.

I also appreciate how open minded you seem to be. You always have something positive to say about the things I've written, and I can just tell that you aren't judging me. My recent life experiences have taught me that mental struggles are real and that we all need a little help from time to time, whether it be therapy, medication, or just extra rest from the things that affect us negatively. I know that you understand this, and I know that you recognize how people evolve over time and hopefully learn to become better versions of themselves. I think that's what human growth and development is all about. It's about going through the various stages of life, falling down numerous times, getting back up, and pushing forward with the new knowledge (and hopefully better coping mechanisms) that we have gained along the way.

I am glad that I decided to go back to school so that I could take this class. Even if I don't continue on with nursing school next spring, it's still part of my five-year plan, and I will take everything I have learned in this class with me into every chapter of my future.

Discussion of Assessment Results

After the disappointing *t*-test results, I was happy to go back through the courses and count up the number and diversity of activities that students completed in the AST condition. It was helpful to see the comparisons in graph form, and I even shared this with my students.

It was also heartening to read student feedback, some of which was shared earlier. In the student comments it was clear that they felt I had acknowledged and accepted their negative feelings (they did not feel judged), and they felt as though they had exercised more autonomy than in an ordinary class.

There was, however, evidence that the online courses were not as structured as they could have been. Several students observed feelings of helplessness at the beginning of the course, though this could have been a natural consequence of students entering the course expecting to be told what to do.

I would absolutely do this again for subsequent online courses, but I would learn from a few of my mistakes. I have organized some of these learnings here so that the reader can avoid making these mistakes themselves.

MISTAKE NUMBER 1: EXPECTATIONS WERE UNCLEAR

I could have done a better job clarifying my expectations for the course. While the two sample learning plans (listed in table 9.1) provided possible pathways for students, students still struggled to find their own direction. To correct this, I will solicit suggestions from students ("Takes Students' Perspective") on how to provide more structure without making students' choices for them.

MISTAKE NUMBER 2: MY UNDERSTANDING OF AST WAS LIMITED

It is clear that I had recently finished reading Deci's *Why We Do What We Do*, because it was very important to me that students had choices. If nothing else, students during this term had many opportunities to direct the path that their individual learning would take.

Table 9.3.   AST strategies included in AST condition

AST Strategy	Included
Takes Students' Perspective	No
Invites Students to Pursue Interests	Yes
Presents Learning in Need-Satisfying Ways	No
Provides Explanatory Rationale	No
Acknowledges Negative Feelings	Yes
Informational, Nonpressuring Language	Yes
Practices Patience	Yes

MISTAKE NUMBER 3: I INTEGRATED TOO FEW AST STRATEGIES

As a consequence of mistake number 2, I integrated too few AST strategies. There is more to AST than choice. Earlier complaints of confusion about expectations could have been followed up by asking for feedback. I also could have explained my rationale for the autonomy-supportive course in my introduction video. Table 9.3 shows the AST strategies I included next to those strategies I ignored.

The strategies I had included were based almost entirely on my teaching style prior to learning about AST. With the help of the workshops in chapters 6 and 7, I could easily make a plan to include the first three AST strategies in an online course. Feedback could be solicited from students at various intervals throughout the term.

Presenting learning activities in need-satisfying ways presented a challenge, because relatedness seems to be less important in the online platform. In subsequent class periods, however, I have had success soliciting personal correspondence from students in the way of letters emailed to the professor (to which I respond personally and honestly). In those classes, online students reported feelings of relation to their professor.

Extra time could be spent assessing how challenged students felt in the course. There was no strategy in place to see if students felt they were being challenged.

Finally, more detailed descriptions of the activities could have been provided along with why I suggested them in the first place.

Conclusion

Looking only at the quantitative data that I collected, I cannot say whether or not the few AST strategies I employed were effective at supporting student autonomy. However, the student feedback, when paired with my own reflections about the course and other metrics of student participation, have provided more than enough data to suggest improvements that can be made to my online courses in the future.

CHAPTER 10

A Case Study of Teacher Transformation

Throughout this book, I have shared many of the changes I have recognized in myself since I began applying the strategies for supporting student autonomy. These have included my patience when listening to students, a growing interest in student affect, and a greater ability to recognize and admit when something I am doing isn't working. But there are also deeper changes that have been going on, too. Changes that I did not realize until reviewing my teaching materials from the past. I discovered, with some horror, just how out of touch I had been with my students—their interests, who they were, and where they were coming from.

For years I have prided myself as being a sympathetic, thoughtful, caring, and supportive college professor. I felt this way even though nothing in my behavior supported such a charitable description. Were you to have asked me seven years ago about how well I supported student autonomy, I would have explained that I wasn't exactly sure, but that it was probably more than a little above average. Figure 10.1 is an illustration that captures the self-report I would have given about my ability to support student autonomy. (The reader will notice how I am willing to grant some room for improvement.)

In the absence of understanding what autonomy support was or how to achieve it, I thought very highly of my abilities as an instructor. I still do. The difference is that now I have empirical evidence that contradicts this rosy perception of my capabilities. I have completed among other inventories the situations in school inventory, which was described in chapter 5. The SIS inventory tells a different story. Despite my pride and arrogance, I learned that my courses were controlling and chaotic. Together, these qualities thwart student autonomy. Figure 10.2 is a graph that more accurately captures where I was with respect to a hypothetical normal distribution of autonomy support across college instructors.

In other words, in 2016 I did not have a very good or honest assessment of my own teaching style. Even as I began integrating the autonomy-supportive strategies into my teaching, I felt as though I was simply doing more of what I had always been doing. But this is sort of like looking for the hidden image in a puzzle. Once you see it, it becomes obvious. You wonder how you could have ever missed it.

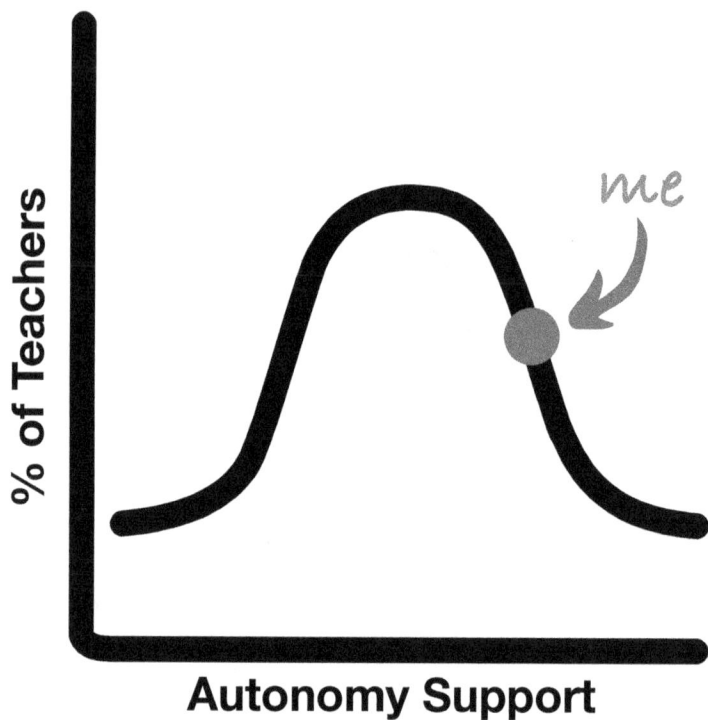

Figure 10.1. My predicted level of autonomy support (2016)

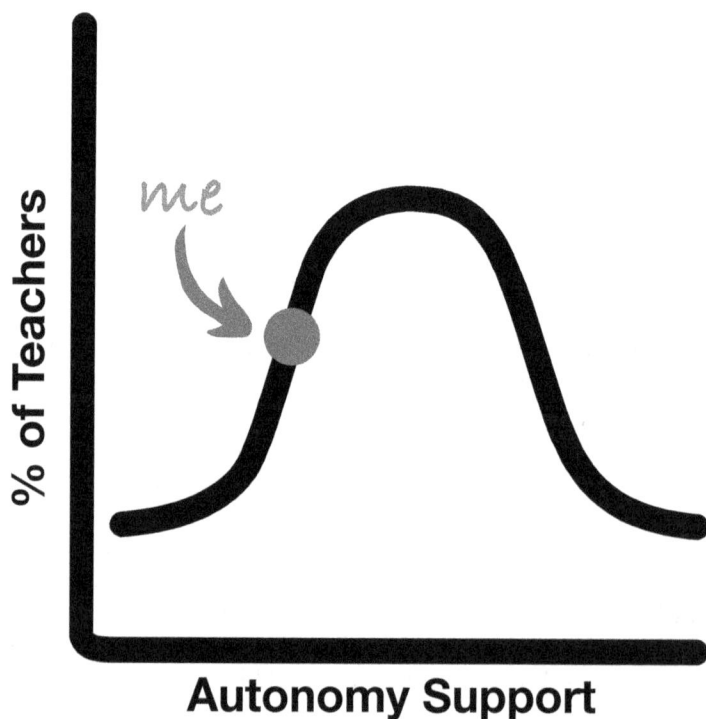

Figure 10.2. Actual level of autonomy support (2021)

When I began taking student feedback seriously, I did not realize that everything about my behavior had already changed. It seemed as though the change was a simple one, such as the type of questions I used while soliciting feedback. I assumed that everything else in my behavior and attitude and awareness was exactly as it had always been. But everything else was not identical. Learning to support student autonomy had transformed the words I used, the way I used them, my expectations, my patience, and my ability to hear what students were saying and how they were saying it.

I appreciate that this will be difficult to understand by listening to me describe it. Because of this, I have decided to share an artifact from my time as an instructor before learning about autonomy-supportive teaching. It is worth mentioning that the artifact was taken from the beginning of my career as a professor, during which I received top marks from students and from my dean and chair. It is a letter that I wrote to my students, which I gave to them on the first day of class back in 2016. It just so happens that the letter was published as the preface to my first book, *Psychologizing: A Personal, Practice-Based Approach to Psychology*, which I published in 2016.[1] There you will find proof that I am not fabricating the artifact you find here. That I published the letter shows how proud I was of my concern and thoughtfulness as a professor. I believed I was a model teacher.

I will share the letter, and then comment on it using my perspective as it has changed since practicing autonomy-supportive teaching. I hope that this contrast will shine a light on the subtle but significant changes that have taken place in me. Changes that have not been conspicuous, but ones that have taken place beneath the surface.

The reader is encouraged to review the letter creatively, keeping in mind the strategies for supporting student autonomy that have been outlined in this book. In what ways does the letter support student autonomy? Fail to support? Notice also my attitude and what it communicates. Do I take my students' perspective? Do I use explanatory rationale? How invitational is my language? How autonomy supportive would you rate me? And so on. Be ruthless.

My 2016 Letter to Students

Welcome to PSYC 101: Introduction to Psychology,

In an "Introduction to [insert academic discipline here]" class, it is the duty of the professor to fill the empty receptacles (the students) that fill her classroom each day with un-erring [insert adjective form of academic discipline here] facts. After forty-two days of receptacle filling, the students, now overflowing with inerrant knowledge, get to regurgitate the memorized gems onto a scantron-sheet, provided they are competent enough to do so. The student-completed scantrons are compared with the correct one, and the students are judged on their understanding. Students who pass are free to build upon their now-verified psychological base; students who fail must survive another forty-two class-periods of receptacle-filling, because it apparently didn't take the first time.

This is not *how this class will be.* The sample "introduction to . . ." course described above is intended to be a caricature of a college class, and not to represent any actual

---

1. The letter is the actual letter given to students. The published version had been edited for general readership.

course. If what I described above in any way resembles experiences of learning that you have had in the past, I am deeply sorry for this. With the exception of ease, I fail to find any merit in this style of learning. My convictions about learning may be expressed by an exemplary educator from nearly a century ago:

> It represents a process by which the [student] learns to become aware of and to evaluate his experience. To do this he cannot begin by studying "subjects" in the hope that some day this information will be useful. On the contrary, he begins by giving attention to situations in which he finds himself, to problems which include obstacles to his self-fulfillment. . . . In this process the teacher finds a new function. She is no longer the oracle who speaks from the platform of authority, but rather the guide, the pointer-outer who also participates in learning in proportion to the vitality and relevancy of her facts and experiences. *In short, my conception of student education is this: a cooperative venture in nonauthoritarian, informal learning, the chief purpose of which is to discover the meaning of experience; a quest of the mind which digs down to the roots of the preconceptions which formulate our conduct; a technique of learning for [students] which makes education coterminous with life and hence elevates living itself to the level of adventurous experiment.* (Lindeman, 1926, p. 160; in Knowles 1989, pp. 73–74; emphasis added)

Some of you are here for some other reason than your own choice. Maybe an advisor signed you up for it or the course is required as a pre-requisite. In these cases, an introduction to psychology is a mere hurdle or roadblock that is preventing you from being where you want to be. Let us acknowledge and accept that this may very well be the case. This is OK. Keep in mind that, while psychology-land might not be your choice-destination, you can use to go where you want to go.

Psychology is an exceedingly broad and intricately nuanced discipline which cannot be sufficiently introduced. You will not leave this class with a firm footing in *the* world of psychology. However, if you engage this course, then you might leave this class with a firm footing in *your* world of psychology. This should be the goal. Indeed, forget about emerging from this class as a psychology expert; focus instead on *taking advantage* of this class in order to facilitate your own goals, motivations, and self-understanding. This may seem a bit unnatural, if not unbelievable, but with a little bit of effort on your part the transition should be manageable.

At this point, I want you to suspend the notion of taking this class. In fact, despite your enrollment status, imagine that you are on the fence about taking this class, and that what you read below along with your experiences in the first few days of class will be the deciding factors on whether or not you stay. (Incidentally, this is how I have always treated the classes that I have taken.)

Class time will be split approximately down the middle between professor-led and student-led activities (the side that the majority falls on will be decided by the class).

Professor-led class time will begin and end each class period. Here is where I get to share *my* footing in psychology. Student-led class-time will consist of, but is not limited to, group workshops, experiments, demonstrations, presentations, and exercises. This is where you get to explore the different ways that you might be able to take advantage of psychology for yourself, and share your interests, successes, and disappointments with one another. In the past, I have had students find ways to take advantage of psychology to develop their acting skills, improve nurse-practitioner bed-side manner, investigate cyber-bullying on social-networking sites, interview a diagnosed schizophrenic, explore the mind of a serial killer, analyze and interpret their own dreams, mediate delinquent behavior in school and in the home, focus during clutch moments in athletics, wean a roommate off of smoking, etc.

As you can see, student-participation will be integral to this class. What you are looking for in the coursework and material, then, are things that relate to *you*, and can be used for *your sake* (or the sake of others in your life). For example, if you read something in the above quote (Lindeman) that you have found interesting, confusing, or even incorrect, then write it down and bring it in to share with classmates and me. This is one way that you connect psychology-land to your everyday life. In time, the rift between what happens in psychology-land and what happens in life will begin to merge. Indeed, what good is psychology if it does not inform your everyday life?

In order to make psychology applicable to your life, you're going to need to identify that which is important to you. This seems relatively straightforward, but it is actually quite complicated. Most students who excel at school—particularly in those whose models are typified by the caricature that began this paper—have become increasingly out of touch with their own interests and desires. These have been replaced by desires imposed upon them by parents, teachers, and maybe other friends. For some of you, this may be characterized by a greater interest in *finishing* school than *being in* school—something of which I am often guilty. So what can you do about it? I trust that after hearing some other students share their interests and concerns related to this class, the uncertainty regarding the application of life will begin to dissolve.

COURSE "DELIVERABLES"

Course deliverables typically include exams, papers, quizzes, and presentations. In the past, I have experimented widely with course deliverable requirements. While I like the idea of allowing the students to choose what will be expected of them, many found this intimidating and strange. As a compromise, I have decided to make this semester's deliverables very straightforward. Simply by attending class and participating in discussions, you will earn 40% of the points for the semester. The rest of your points will be made during two essay examinations (which will build directly off of class discussions), as well as weekly quizzes.

DESIRE2LEARN

While it may not always seem to be the case, we can assume D2L has been implemented as a resource that is capable of providing the "utmost information from the simplest apparatus" (Whitehead, 1929, p. 17). For the purposes of this course, D2L will serve as a resource intermediary between myself and you. For instance, you will find the rubrics to possible assignments, subdiscipline-specific readings, links to videos and websites, and copies of documents like the one you are reading.

A benefit of D2L as a resource intermediary will be the reduction of printed-paper waste (and cost—8 cents a page!). With your help, we may be able to complete the semester with limited paper use.

Because it has been newly implemented, we will all have to be patient with its use as we familiarize ourselves with it.

BE YOURSELF

Finally, I am not asking you to participate in this class in any other way than as yourself. I will hold myself to the same standard. To paraphrase Gestalt therapist Fritz Perls, I will be me and you be you; I am not in this class to satisfy your needs (though I may try), just as you are not in this class to satisfy my needs. If, in being ourselves, we should happen to develop one another's understanding, it will be wonderful.

With sincerity,

Patrick M Whitehead, PhD

My 2022 Analysis of the 2016 Letter to Students

THE LETTER IS LONG

This letter to my students is nearly 1,500 words long, which works out to 2.5 single-spaced pages. This is comparable in length to an essay. It is less of a letter, and more of a reading assignment. It would not surprise me if the majority of students skimmed the letter or skipped it entirely. I found myself getting bored trying to read it before writing this section.

THE LETTER IS FORMATTED USING HEADINGS

It appears as though my letter has followed the formatting guidelines of the American Psychological Association (APA). This makes it about as personal and candid as the stenographer's account of a courtroom proceeding.

THERE IS A BLOCK QUOTE

The letter has a long quote, complete with citation and analysis. See previous comment.

THE LETTER IS NOT WRITTEN FROM THE STUDENTS' PERSPECTIVE

It is clear to me that this letter has not been written from my students' perspective. It would also be difficult to say that the letter was written from a teacher's perspective.

The letter has conformed itself to APA style guidelines, and follows an analytical line of thinking. It is therefore fair to say that the letter has been written from a scholar's perspective. This communicates to the recipients of the letter that its author has not bothered to remove his scholarly writing cap.

If the letter were written from the students' perspective, then I would expect it to be much shorter than it is. Half a page or less. I also would not have opened with an example of the opposite of what students can expect. Doing so is unnecessarily confusing to the student who is no doubt eager to figure out the structure of the course, the requirements, and the preferences of their instructor. Instead, what the reader learns is that their instructor is misleading, cryptic, and sarcastic.

The vocabulary in the letter is unnecessarily obtuse. I use words like "inerrant" and "regurgitate" and "exceedingly" and "intricately." Sure, these are words that college students probably know, but this isn't the SAT. None of those words are necessary, and there is no place for them in a personal letter written to first-year college students.

The outline of the class is the product of the instructor's imagination. I explain how there will be student-led activities, which I clarify with the following: "the side that the majority falls on will be decided by the class." The majority of what? The student will probably be thinking, "so I'm going to have to participate by doing something that my instructor doesn't even understand."

I would expect a student to be confused by the letter, and therefore uncertain about what to expect in the class. In the language of AST, the letter is chaotic.

STUDENTS ARE EXPECTED TO BE GUIDED BY INTRINSIC MOTIVATION

I suspect that a student who reads this letter, provided they are able to follow its plodding narrative, will feel bad about their reliance on extrinsic motivators. The letter makes it clear that the best students are the ones who wake up with the personal goal of attending a course in general psychology. Students who have been motivated to satisfy the expectations of parents, teachers, and others, which represents the majority of students in my experience, will feel like they are doing it the wrong way. This judgment is communicated without any real alternative explanation given, which is likely to make the whole situation feel hopeless to a first-time student.

In terms of the three principle motivators defined by self-determination theorists, there is little support for autonomy, competence, or relatedness. There is no gauge for the experience and understanding that students will bring with them to class. They are expected, for example, to facilitate their personal goals, but there is no talk about exploring what those goals might be. I know that many eighteen-year-olds have not thought through their personal goals, but have swallowed the goals of their parents, friends, or the media. The letter implies, however, that these sources of motivation are wrong. In retrospect, I can see that I did not understand the role of motivation in the facilitation of learning. To me it was either intrinsic motivation, which seemed magical and unpredictable to me at the time, or nothing. I didn't understand the nuances and growth potential of extrinsic sources of motivation.

There is also no invitation in the letter for how students might relate to other students. This was because, at the time, I was inexperienced in giving students this opportunity. I of course hoped that they would relate, but I had no idea what that might look like. Therefore I could give no examples of doing so in my letter. Instead, I completely ignored the bit about relating. I'm not sure I understood its importance, anyhow. You could read this letter and be justified in thinking that each student would work in a closet by themselves all semester long.

THERE IS LITTLE EXPLANATORY RATIONALE

The letter does a poor job of explaining why the course is structured the way that it is, and why the activities have been designed the way that they are. Indeed, there is little description of the structure or activities aside from that some will be instructor centered and others will be student centered.

Anything that might be called "explanatory rationale" has less to do with explaining and more to do with defending. I am implying, for example, how this style of teaching is inspired, and it has been around for one hundred years. But the reader is wondering all the while, "what *is* the style, and why does it matter to me?" This remains unclear.

THERE IS NO ROOM FOR AFFECT

To be fair to my slightly younger self, it is impossible to acknowledge negative affect in the absence of interaction. This does not mean, however, that it would be impossible to indicate that there will be room for emotion and feelings and concerns and so on in the classroom.

It is not clear from the letter that its author has an emotional life. He writes like a fountain of possibly relevant information. I can imagine that the letter has been written by a brain—specifically the left occipital cortex—that has been hooked up to a monitor. It is almost as if the course described in the letter will be 100% intellectual. There is talk of feelings and disappointments, but these are couched in a way as to designate them psychological phenomena—that is, feelings become concepts to be covered in the curriculum.

IT'S MY WAY OR THE HIGHWAY

I remember writing the bit about students "being on the fence" with regard to their enrollment status. I thought about how cool it probably made me seem. I imagined students thinking, "Wow, this guy is totally fine with me dropping his class."

This was my attempt to give students an important option in the way that their general psychology course had been designed. While I was not willing to change my own course structure (which, we've seen, was very chaotic), I wanted students to see that they could still choose the course they would wind up taking. I hoped that this offer meant that students would only stick around if they truly liked the course design.

I had assumed, incorrectly it would turn out, that students could use their smartphone to switch out of my course and into a comparable one. That was how easy it had been for me, except that I didn't have a smartphone while I was in college. In order for my students to drop my course and add another, they would have to fill out a form and have it signed by their advisor. The advisor would have to email the registrar to have the student's registration hold removed and the new course approved. If approved, the registrar would need written consent from the new instructor that it would be okay for the student to be added to the course.

It isn't a perfect system, but it is the system we have in place. Moreover, it is the only system our students have available to them, and I had failed to appreciate the difficulty of the hurdles they had already managed to navigate by simply registering for my course to begin with.

The reality of my offer was that students didn't really have the option of withdrawing from my course. So in my take it or leave it proposition, their only real choice was to take it.

I could just as easily have written, "I am inflexible with the structure and requirements of this course, and you will find a way to live with that."

SELECTIVE PATIENCE

Hidden in between the lines is a promise that the author of the letter will be impatient. Commands such as "should," "need," "have to," and so on are sprinkled throughout the letter. In other words, the instructor will be patient and sympathetic provided the student follows all of the rules.

IT ISN'T ALL BAD

As fun as it is to criticize my younger teaching self, I think it would be unfair to suggest that I did everything wrong. After all, I don't want college instructors who are reading this to feel as though I am criticizing them. If you are reading this book or others like it, then you are already doing much to support your students and improve your teaching.

I cannot overlook the fact that I took the time to write a letter to my students, a practice that I have been doing for the past ten years. The letter is not the obligatory syllabus; it is something extra. Students who receive the letter will think, at the very least, that their instructor has tried to meet students where they are—that their instructor has tried to step away from the lectern and relate to his students as a person. The students will learn that their instructor is clumsy and awkward in this regard, but that is still a personal look at who their instructor is.

A Digital Letter Written to an Online Health Psychology Course in 2022

Having assessed the letter I wrote to my general psychology students in fall 2016, we may now compare it to a letter written approximately one year after putting the AST principles to work in my courses. The letter was not titled "Introductory Letter." It went by a title that I imagined would be catchier and more immediately relevant. That title was, "But What Am I Supposed to Be Doing?" Here is the letter:

> Dear Student,
>
> In an ordinary online class, I understand that the instructor has created maybe 16 quizzes and 16 discussion posts and 16 assignments that you have to go through and complete. These have been designed in the hopes that, by going through all of these steps, you might transform into a different person—an educated person.
>
> I don't think that that process is beneficial for students, mostly because it is terribly boring, but also because students usually forget 70% of what they've learned in a few weeks' time.
>
> So, instead, I'm inviting you to choose something (or somethings) that you think would be a worthwhile way of spending 16 weeks when your objective is "personal health and well-being."
>
> **"How will I do this?"**
>
> Begin by taking a deep breath. What I am asking you to do probably seems overwhelming. You are not used to making these choices on your own—at least not in the context of a university course. (You of course make choices on your own all the time when you are not in school.)
>
> *Is there anything medically or physically that you would like to work on?*
>
> Would you like to lose weight? Gain weight? Exercise more? Be less stressed? Be happier? Etc. (I can help you find resources for all of these.)
>
> *Do you want to help anybody else be healthier or happier?*
>
> You can apply the same principles and strategies to other people.
>
> *Is there anything academically you would like to work on?*
>
> Do you want to improve your reading ability? Your writing? Your presentation skills? Interpersonal skills? Critical thinking?
>
> *Is there anything you would like to memorize?*
>
> Would you like to know all about chronic pain? STDs? AIDS? Head injuries? Alzheimer's Disease?
>
> **Still having trouble deciding?**
>
> I have written a short manual over the winter break where I introduce three health psychology interventions, three health psychology research methods, and three health psychology assessments. They are:
>
> - *Health Assessments:* Quality of Life Inventory, Sense of Coherence, and Life Changes (Stress) Inventory
> - *Health Interventions:* Mindfulness-Based Stress Reduction, Positive Psychology, Easy Exercise
> - *Health Research:* Single Participant Experiments, Ethnography, Case Study
>
> I am looking forward to seeing what we can create together!
> —dr. w

GENERAL OBSERVATIONS

The letter is much shorter. It is 360 words compared to 1,455 in the earlier letter. Reading over it just now, there wasn't enough time for me to get bored.

Reading the letters in sequence like this, it is clear that I have a tendency to begin course introductions with the opposite of what students are to expect. I probably developed this preference during years and years of reading the French philosopher Maurice Merleau-Ponty, who was famous for giving long and looping descriptions that he would later contradict. He was also, by total coincidence, called "the philosopher of ambiguity." In the 2022 letter, however, this what-not-to-expect introduction was shortened to two sentences, and these are followed by an unambiguous statement of my opinion about ordinary course design.

The vocabulary in the 2022 letter is much simpler. There are no $100 words. The letter sounds like it was written by a human being who has convictions and opinions, and who has taken the time to consider the course from the perspective of other human beings.

The bulk of the letter is organized around questions that I can imagine students might wish to ask. These are questions that students might not think of right away, but, once they've read them, will realize that they, too, have that question. The answers I provide take into consideration the affect that probably accompanies each question. That is to say, the answers respond to the question as well as the questioner, thereby acknowledging possible nervousness or anxiety on the part of the student.

The letter suggests plenty of structure in the course. Students are given lots of detailed options. They are invited to design their own path or, if that seems too daunting, take a predetermined pathway.

There is limited explanatory rationale. I suspect, however, that students did not need to hear rationale for promoting personal health and well-being, which was the stated objective of the course. In practice, students explored many creative interpretations of this objective and outlets for its achievement. Many did so in ways that I couldn't have predicted, but that nevertheless met the desired outcome. (I have found that the more flexibly I allow students to explore methods for meeting desired outcomes, the more impressed I become with student aptitude, and the more likely I am to extend flexibility to future groups of students.)

I have imagined possible learning and personal development goals that students might have in the hopes of providing optimal challenges in areas of growth that the students perceive as worthwhile. While there are no explicit instructions for relating with the instructor or others in class, students are encouraged to explore the relationship between the course objective and other people in their lives. I predicted that students would use the health inventories to explore stress and quality of life in their family members. But this didn't happen nearly as much as students who identified relatedness goals for their own well-being and life satisfaction ("getting out more," "getting out of my comfort zone," "going on at least one date per month"). Of course! Relatedness factors are among the most potent explored by cardiac psychologists, which are physicians who recognize the psychological factors related to chronic heart disease (Allan & Fisher, 2011).

In the letter, I provide plenty of information about possible learning and personal development activities, as well as directions for finding more information in the online course. While there are clearly objectives that would need to be met, the methods for doing so are left open ended.

Perhaps it is worth mentioning at this point that I did not draft this letter with the seven principles of AST in mind. I do recall trying to consider my students' perspective while I was writing it. If memory serves, I wrote the letter a day after the class began, because I imagined that students were staring with uncertainty at all of the course materials and documents and folders they had confronted in the online classroom. I imagined them asking the title question, namely, "What is it that I am supposed to be doing?"

Conclusion
TROUBLESHOOTING PROBLEMS
AND LOOKING FORWARD

Some Instructors Will Do This Naturally

During my workshop, I had the privilege of visiting several classrooms and discussing with faculty the strengths and weaknesses of the learning climate they facilitated. One observation that stood out among the others was how common it seemed for instructors to have already been using the AST strategies before ever learning about the research support. Many of the strategies, it seems, are intuitive.

In a biology classroom that I was observing, for example, Dr. L welcomed each of her students by name. One young woman came in a few minutes late and sat down without making eye contact. Dr. L paused and waited until the student looked up.

"You having a bad day?" Dr. L asked. The question was neither sarcastic nor accusatory.

The student shrugged.

Dr. L waited. So did the other students. So did I, their guest visitor. I did not get the feeling that Dr. L and the other students were waiting for this grumpy student to correct her behavior. There was no judgment involved. The social environment was one in which it would be okay for this student to complain or argue or cry or continue fidgeting with her phone.

"Do you need a hug?" asked Dr. L. There was no trace of sarcasm in her voice.

The student paused, then nodded. Dr. L wasted no time in walking over to the student and giving her a real, full-body hug.

The student sat back down, and Dr. L continued with the activity she had started.

This example is not intended to demonstrate how to acknowledge and accept negative affect, though it does so brilliantly. It is intended to show one professor's version of acknowledging and accepting negative affect. I have never hugged a student, and don't think I would be able to do so without communicating my own discomfort.

As I watched Dr. L interact with her students throughout the hour and 15 minutes of the class, I got the impression that she was not trying something new. I was witnessing her own unique way of relating to her students in the context of teaching. Even before reading about supporting student autonomy, Dr. L was a master at welcoming students into her classroom. I did not feel the slightest bit uncomfortable or out of place, even though I was a stranger who, I later learned, had accidentally sat in Meaghan's seat.

When I asked her about it afterward, Dr. L was surprised. She explained that she didn't think she was doing anything remarkable or unusual. It was just who she was as a professor. What Dr. L taught me was that it is possible to create an emotionally warm and accepting classroom.

This was something I had never experienced before in a classroom. Not in one of my own classrooms, or in any of the many dozens of classrooms I had been in as a student. Dr. L had created an environment of comfort and familiarity. It was almost as if close friends were getting together for their weekly visit. All by itself, this social and emotional feeling of being welcomed into the classroom provided profound autonomy support. I had to hold back my own interest in speaking up and participating in class. (I am confident that the others would have listened carefully and would have entertained anything I had shared.)

But this didn't mean that Dr. L was a natural at each of the seven strategies for supporting student autonomy. When we discussed areas where she felt weak or inexperienced, she talked about how she could work on patience, and how she might optimize the level of difficulty across students who have a variety of skill levels.

Another professor was a natural when it came to giving explanatory rationale. This was Dr. D, chair of the department of teacher education and long-time teacher. "I don't understand how you can ask kids to do something without explaining why they're doing it," Dr. D explained. "Do you?" she continued. "Am I crazy? I just don't see how that's possible. You have to explain it or else they won't want to do it. I certainly wouldn't want to do it. Would you?"

When we discussed explanatory rationale, it became clear that Dr. D already had great familiarity with it. She and other faculty had been working with a strategy called "TiLT," which stands for "transparency in learning and teaching" (Akella et al., 2022). This strategy called for teachers to show in advance the cognitive steps for solving a problem, along with rationale for why each step is necessary or what it accomplishes.

After reading about TiLT on the TiLT Higher Ed website (tilthighered.com) I decided that "giving explanatory rationale" was identical to TiLT. "Nope!" said Dr. D. "I see them as different." She explained how TiLT is formulaic—how every problem has to be broken down into so many steps, whether or not that was how the problems were most intuitively solved. "Yes, they both deal with answering why certain steps are included," said Dr. D, "but I prefer to share practical reasons for doing what we do. Don't you?"

As you were reading over the seven strategies, you have probably realized that you were already doing a few of them without thinking. If this was the case, then you are already partway there. While you might want to skip over the strategies you do well, I would recommend spending time on them anyhow. This is because it is helpful to focus on strengths rather than always focusing on your weaknesses. This was the model of education that Howard Gardner had in mind when he described his eight intelligences.

When you see the pinwheel of Gardner's (2011) multiple intelligences, you might think that the end goal is the Renaissance person—a sort of Leonardo Da Vinci who has an even balance of all eight intelligence styles. But that wasn't Gardner's goal. Gardner wished to see schools offer specializations based on intelligence styles—musical schools for the musically gifted, visual arts schools for the artistically gifted, and so on. Gardner was unhappy with the singular emphasis on language, logic, and mathematics in schools. This only allowed the students with those gifts to thrive.

Remember also what I explained in chapter 2, which is that AST is a Gestalt—excellence at any one of the strategies indicates excellence at the others. By strengthening any of the strategies, you are strengthening the others as well.

After interacting with faculty at all stages of their careers, I have come to appreciate a diversity of instructional gifts that faculty have.

Anticipating Problems

I thought it might be helpful to see some of the problems that my colleagues and I ran into when we began using AST in our classrooms, and how we solved those problems. That way you and your colleagues might have an idea of what to expect when implementing the AST strategies yourselves.

THE NEED FOR STRUCTURE

I realized the need for structure while organizing my first AST workshop for fellow faculty. What I had hoped was that faculty would find their own way into learning how to support student autonomy if all that I did was provide them with the same resources that I had found helpful. This proved to be a mistake.

Here is what I did: I gave all faculty participants around 5,000 pages of peer-reviewed articles and book chapters, five self-report assessments, one classroom visitation form, and a summary essay like chapter 2 of this book. We arranged to meet every other week to discuss insights from the readings, and any problems the workshop participants had experienced with the application of those insights to their classrooms.

But I had failed to take my workshop participants' point of view.

Included among the participants in the workshop was a nontenure track instructor who was teaching three courses at our university, three courses at a nearby technical school, and two courses at a professional school that specializes in offering college credits to high school students. A second participant was teaching six writing-intensive courses at our university. A third was teaching four courses, serving as program coordinator for their department and coordinator for a new minor, and belonged to a dozen or so university committees. A fourth participant was codirector of a center on campus, chair of their department, a member of dozens of university committees, and taught two courses and conducted teacher supervisions. And so on. The participants were extremely busy.

They were eager to learn ways to support their students' autonomy, but they were already so busy with their obligations that they had little time to devote to reading through the piles of resources I had provided. These resources sat mostly untouched.

In a candid conversation with one of the participants, I shared how I was disappointed in how the workshop was getting along. I imagined that the participants had read through the materials, but that they did not like what they had read. During our meetings, again I imagined, the participants had nothing to share because they felt threatened by the principles of AST. I was imagining a conflict between teaching philosophies.

Because they were gracious and courageous, this participant confided in me that they did not feel like the participants had read through and then rejected the AST resources. They described what they thought was a more reasonable explanation, which was that the participants were already so buried in responsibilities that they had been unable to read—let alone meditate on the perceived value of—the articles and book chapters. The quiet disinterest during our meetings was on account of participants having not done the reading.

And why should they have done the reading? Like the students we teach, the faculty participants were busy with jobs, relationships, medical problems, financial issues, vacations, fights with bosses and colleagues, and so on. Even though they wanted to grow as teachers, they struggled to find the time. Sure, they could find an odd hour here and 20 minutes there, but why sacrifice this precious free time when doing so would only mean *possibly* making it through a 25-page journal article, which might not even prove helpful.

Thinking together with this considerate and honest participant, we developed a new focus for the workshop. Instead of the nondirective approach that I had engineered, we could follow extremely specific and structured applications. That is, instead of the gentle push to follow their own intuition and intrinsic regulation, participants were given guided activities to follow. Each week, participants would be invited to try a new practice, which they could follow as easily as the recipe on the back of Duncan Hines box.

In the language of AST, my original workshop design had been chaotic. It lacked structure. Providing a structure-free workshop sounds wonderful from the vantage point of liberal education, because it means that the participants could make of the workshop whatever they wished. But a structure-free workshop, though unrestrained, is sort of like entering a giant warehouse with rows and rows of shelves arranged in no particular order, and then trying to locate the sandwich bags. My participants could either spend nine or ten hours leafing through the resources in search of something helpful, or they could tend to their more pressing personal and professional obligations.

My colleagues agreed to participate in the workshop because they had a clear idea of what they hoped to achieve. They were guided by a personal desire to transform their identities as faculty in order to become more autonomy supportive. Due to the lack of structure, however, participants were unable to find a clear direction through the materials and toward their goals.

By providing structure and telling these participants what to do, I was worried that I might be limiting their autonomy. But, by holding back on structure, I was ignoring the evidence in the very resources I was providing. I was ignoring the robust detail that structure supports autonomy (Jang et al., 2010). In other words, I could provide sample applications without becoming a dictator. After all, I wasn't going to be making demands on them, nor was I offering them incentives for doing as they were told.

I sent the workshop participants the following message:

> I have decided to make a substantial process change to the workshop. Instead of finding your own way through the resources I have provided, for the second half of the workshop I will give you specific homework activities. The homework activities will be simple and straightforward, and they will ask you to implement ONE strategy for supporting student autonomy.

Moving forward, I provided easy-to-follow in-class activities that participating faculty could use. The investment of time it asked of participants was to be minimal, and the context of these practices (that is, the classroom) allowed participants to experience the impact of AST immediately and directly. And thus, the practical workshop style was developed.

As we creatively implemented AST strategies into our classrooms, we came across a few problems. They are problems that an interested college instructor may face in their attempts to support student autonomy. A description of those problems follows.

LOGISTICAL PROBLEMS WITH ADOPTING AUTONOMY-SUPPORTIVE TEACHING

There was a catch-22 (an infinite loop of contradicting premises) with the process of learning and implementing new teaching strategies during an academic semester. In order to really learn and understand a new teaching strategy, an instructor needs to apply it to their courses. But if an instructor waits until the courses have already begun to apply a new strategy, then it is already too late.

I can imagine a number of ways around this problem:

1. Instructors can practice the strategies in make believe classroom contexts. For example, they can plan a hypothetical activity for a hypothetical class. The problem with this is that they cannot observe how their students respond and then make corrections as necessary.
2. Instructors can practice the strategies in courses they have already started. Once a class and all of its requirements have been introduced, it is nearly impossible to go back and revise them with student input. In other words, once the class has begun it is too late to consider students' perspective except as a consideration after the fact. For better or worse, this was the strategy we used.
3. Workshops could take place in advance of the semester (perhaps at the end of a previous semester, during holiday break, and so on). But it is difficult for instructors to take a workshop seriously when it is occurring during their holiday or during a stressful period of a semester that wouldn't otherwise be impacted. I also seriously doubt that I would have had many participants if I conducted an intensive eight-hour workshop sometime between winter commencement and the holidays.

There are plenty of models for organizing teaching workshops. For example, Cheon and others (2020) have outlined a three-part process for introducing the strategies for AST, integrating them with structure, and reinforcing them. This works out to a factorial equation of around 36 steps, where each strategy is integrated with an element of course structure, and is then mutually supported by the other five strategies. They encourage instructors to reflect on the course changes before, during, and after implementation.

As became clear during my workshop, university faculty are already laden with many responsibilities—teaching, research, advising, mentoring, student clubs, and administrative work—to say nothing of responsibilities at home as a parent, spouse, or sibling. This makes scheduling and carrying out intensive workshops difficult.

CONFUSION ABOUT WHAT THE STRATEGIES ENTAIL

As I have shared in my introduction to the strategies for supporting student autonomy, one of the most significant personal realizations I had concerned accepting negative feelings. I shared with excitement the impact I had experienced with empathizing with my students.

But I quickly found that I was alone in my opinion. "I don't think some emotions are helpful," said one participant. "Why would I accept something that is unhelpful?"

Another participant agreed. "What am I supposed to do if a student is frustrated? Just let her be frustrated? Even if I can listen to her and help her solve her problem?"

It was clear that these two participants felt threatened when it was suggested that they acknowledge and accept negative affect. Because of this, they felt it necessary to defend themselves. I could almost see each participant digging in their heels, ready for a fight.

I acknowledged their frustration. "You're not sure it is always necessary to acknowledge and accept the negative affect of your students?"

Their guards came down a little. "I can see how it would be helpful in some cases," said one participant. "Like I had this one girl who was really upset about something, and I could see that she didn't want to talk about it so I didn't make her. Well she came up to me after class the following week and told me that her closest friend had been abused by a family member."

"Wow," I said. "It sounds to me like you understood this student's anger and fear. That you didn't think that she should just suck it up and keep it from interfering with learning."

"Of course it would interfere with learning!" the workshop participant said.

"And you acknowledged that, too," I observed.

This professor thought that acknowledging and accepting negative affect meant ignoring emotion—letting student affect sort of work itself out. I recognized my role in this misunderstanding, as I had described the practice that I most needed to learn, which was how to stop rescuing students when they were in distress.

As a psychology professor, I had found myself giving advice when it wasn't being solicited. A student would complain because they wanted to complain, but I would rush in and say, "Here is how you could solve that problem." This was my indirect way of telling students that they were not okay unless they were relaxed, comfortable, and focused on the task at hand. In other words, it was my way of refusing to accept students' negative feelings.

In comparison, the story told by my workshop participant showed a great deal of empathy and understanding and concern for her students. This, I believe, was one of her gifts as an instructor. It is not one of mine. My empathy is about as warm and as comforting as a brass toilet seat in the Yukon Territories of northern Canada.

DISAGREEMENT ABOUT THE TEACHABILITY OF CERTAIN STRATEGIES

It would be a waste of time to describe a helpful teaching strategy if the strategy was impossible to learn. This would sort of be like giving a lecture on how useful it is to have a photographic memory when it comes to learning student names. Very few people have a photographic memory, and it isn't a skill that can be practiced.

So what about the strategies for supporting student autonomy? Can they be learned? The referenced literature suggests that instructors can improve on the autonomy support that they provide, so it would be logical to assume that the skills that represent autonomy support can be learned (see Reeve & Cheon, 2021). But a few workshop participants didn't think so. They didn't believe, for example, that a person could learn patience. "You've either got it, or you don't."

This long-time professor was outspoken about the benefits of patience for the teacher. They believed patience to be essential to quality teaching. They did not, however, believe that it could be taught to another person.

There are a lot of ways to define patience or to recognize it in the classroom. A simple measure could be the amount of time an instructor is willing to wait after asking a question. We have all been in those situations where an anxious administrator or colleague asks for a show of hands or for an example from the audience, but then gives up in embarrassment after two or three seconds. Would it be possible for this person to practice waiting for five seconds? Ten seconds? Of course. We could even measure the improvement in patience.

I think what this workshop participant meant had more to do with a personality style, which is less malleable than a classroom behavior.

I was shocked to learn that my workshop participants thought of me as a patient facilitator. For decades I have identified as an impatient sort of person. But I have practiced waiting and listening and giving students (or workshop participants) the space they needed to develop their own ideas and their own understanding. I was delighted that these behavioral changes were noticeable, because that meant that I had changed them!

EXTERNAL PRESSURES TO BE CONTROLLING

In the introduction I described the cultural belief that controlling teachers are better teachers. Students, faculty, and administration believe, deep down, that a strict, authoritarian, and demanding instructor is better than a flexible, patient, and empathic instructor. This belief is upheld despite enormous evidence to the contrary. Therefore, it was easy to understand when some of the faculty participants reported feeling pressured to abandon the autonomy-supportive strategies in favor of more controlling methods.

A Call for More Research on AST in Higher Education

I would like to end this book with a challenge: If you have used AST and you work in higher education, then share how it went by publishing your results. It doesn't matter if you are a part-time instructor at a technical school or a professor emeritus at a top-tier institution: If you applied the strategies for supporting student (or fellow faculty or administrator or janitorial staff) autonomy, then let the rest of us know.

If it hasn't been clear, I don't typically follow the rules. When I learn about a new strategy, I like to take it apart in order to see how it works. When doing so, I sometimes rebuild it in a different way—a way that seems like it works better. In particular, I have been interested in using autonomy support in nondirective courses. These are courses where students are given wide measures of freedom to determine course structure, objectives, and so forth. I have found autonomy support to work very nicely in situations where students are uncomfortable choosing the direction and speed of a course. In a class just yesterday my students had decided that they were finished exploring their first course objective, which was preparing for what they were going to do after graduating. My inclination was to hand them reflection sheets right then, but I decided to get their feedback first. I asked them how they thought we might wrap the subject up, and listened attentively to their suggestions. Within three minutes, nearly every student confessed that they weren't sure what to include in a recommendation letter (I had encouraged them to write a letter on their own behalf). We spoke about it for the rest of the hour, shared resources, and built another class period around workshopping what they had started.

Other faculty have used autonomy support alongside the principles of grit (passion and determination) and locus of control. While the field could certainly benefit from randomized control trials testing AST in each of the following contexts, there is also a need for program evaluations. That is to say, it is helpful to hear what the introduction of AST into courses has done for other faculty—faculty whose students or whose school or whose discipline might represent your own. These are program evaluations, in which any number of research methods could be employed. Spauling (2013) describes six strategies for higher education program evaluation. Depending on your institution, ethical review may be required.

I am personally interested in seeing AST applied in a number of contexts, which I share here.

AST in Large Lecture Halls

At many universities—even the small ones—enormous class sizes are common for introductory courses. Whether such courses are ideal for student learning, lecture halls are the reality for many instructors. In chapter 3, for example, medical students (Duguid et al., 2020) confessed that large lecture courses were standard for the majority of foundation courses such as physiology. But, as Neufield & Malin (2020, 2021) have observed, AST is still suitable for large classes. Implementation of the strategies in a large hall would likely look quite a bit different from implementation in courses with 15 or fewer students.

Maybe you have taught high-enrollment lecture courses, and have tried to integrate the seven AST strategies. What did this look like? What sorts of changes were necessary? What problems arose and how did you fix them? How did your students respond? What might you do differently if you tried it again?

Asynchronous Online Courses

In chapters 3 and 10, I have shared data and recommendations about implementing AST in asynchronous online courses. This evidence suggests that AST would make a valuable strategy for asynchronous courses, but that the results are less robust than when implemented in face-to-face courses. With so few studies, it is difficult to understand precisely how to support student autonomy, competence, and relatedness online. I think we would all benefit as instructors if others shared their strategies for practicing AST in their online courses, as well as what worked and what did not. It is my opinion that a second book could be written on AST in online and asynchronous courses.

Professional and Organizational Development

The importance for autonomy support at the administrative level was briefly mentioned in the introduction. There I shared evidence that controlling administrative styles led to controlling teaching styles, which led to student indifference and externalization of learning objectives in the classroom. But how might this be done most effectively?

I suspect that workshops, much like the ones outlined in this book, could be designed for college administrators—department chairs, college deans, vice presidents, provosts, presidents, and so on. I predict that by training faculty and staff in an autonomy-supportive way, those faculty and staff would increasingly internalize the institutional goals and objectives, and they would experience great satisfaction and psychological well-being while doing so.

This could begin with professional development for faculty and staff (ordinary and required trainings, tutorials, or workshops) and could extend to the annual job evaluation and assessment strategies.

References

Aelterman, N., Vansteenkiste, M., Soenens, B., Fontaine, J., Haerens, L., Delrue, J., & Reeve, J. (2019). Toward a fine-grained understanding of the components of need-supportive and need-thwarting teaching: The merits of a gradual approach. *Journal of Educational Psychology, 111*(3), 497–521.

Aelterman, N., Vansteenkiste, M., Van Keer, H., de Meyer, J., Van den Berghe, L., Haerens, L. (2013). Development and evaluation of a training on need-supportive teaching in physical education: Qualitative and quantitative findings. *Teaching and Teacher Education, 29,* 64–75.

Akella, D., Paudel, L., & Wickramage, N. (2022). *Integrating transparency in learning and teaching (TILT): An effective tool for providing equitable opportunity in higher education.* IGI Global.

Allan, R., & Fisher, J. (2011). *Heart and mind: The practice of cardiac psychology.* American Psychological Association.

Baars, B. J. (1986). *The cognitive revolution in psychology.* New York: Guilford Press.

Baumeister, R. F., & Leary, M. R. (1995). The need to belong: Desire for interpersonal attachments as a fundamental human motivation. *Psychological Bulletin, 117*(3), 497–529.

Beck, A. M., & Diehr, A. J. (2017). The effects of teaching fitness in an autonomy-supportive style. *American Journal of Health Studies, 32*(4), 201–207.

Bonneville-Roussy, A., Hruska, E., & Trower, H. (2020). Teaching music to support students: How autonomy-supportive music teachers increase students' well-being. *Journal of Research in Music Education, 68*(1), 97–119.

Breland, K., & Breland, M. (1961). The misbehavior of organisms. *American Psychologist, 16*(11), 681–684.

Bunce, L., & King, N. (2019). Experiences of autonomy support in learning and teaching among black and minority students at university. *The Psychology of Education Review, 43*(2), 2–8.

Cain, D. J. (2003). Advancing humanistic psychology and psychotherapy: Some challenges and proposed solutions. *Journal of Humanistic Psychology, 43*(3), 10–41.

Chen, K., & Jang, S. (2010). Motivation in online learning: Testing a model of self-determination theory. *Computers in human behavior.*

Cheon, S. H., Reeve, J., & Vansteenkiste, M. (2020). When teachers learn how to provide classroom structure in an autonomy-supportive way: Benefits to teachers and their students. *Teaching and Teacher Education, 90,* 1–12. https://doi.org/10.1016/j.tate.2019.103004.

Clifford, M. M. (1990). Students need challenge, not easy success. *Educational Leadership.* September, 22–26.

Codina, N., Valenzuela, R., Pestana, J. V., & Gonzalez-Conde, J. (2018). Relations between student procrastination and teaching styles: Autonomy-supportive and controlling. *Frontiers in Psychology, 9*(809), 1–7.

Covington, M. V., von Hoene, L. M., & Voge, D. J. (2017). *Life beyond grades: Designing college courses to promote intrinsic motivation.* Cambridge: Cambridge University Press.

Criss, S., Grant, L., Henderson, N., Sease, K., Fumo, M., & Stetler, C. (2021). Changing attitudes about spanking: A mixed-methods study of a positive parenting intervention. *Journal of Child and Family Studies, 30,* 2504–2515.

Deci, R., & Flaste, R. (1995). *Why we do what we do: Understanding self-motivation.* Penguin.

Duckworth, A. (2016). *Grit: The power of passion and perseverance.* New York: Scribner.

Duguid, J., Duguid, L., & Bryan, J. (2020). Students' perspective on how instructor autonomy-support mediate their motivation and psychological well-being. *Medical Teacher, 42*(12), 1430.

Dweck, C. (2006). *Mindset: The new psychology of success.* New York: Random House.

Elkins, D. N. (2007). Why humanistic psychology lost its power and influence in American psychology: Implications for advancing humanistic psychology. *Journal of Humanistic Psychology, 49,* 267–291.

Emdin, C. (2016). *For white folks who teach in the hood . . . and the rest of y'all too: Reality pedagogy and urban education.* Boston: Beacon Press.

Erikson, E. (1994). *Identity and the life cycle.* New York: W. W. Norton & Company.

Eyler, J. R. (2018). *How humans learn: The science and stories behind effective college teaching.* Morgantown: West Virginia University Press.

Frankl, V. E. (1959). *Man's search for meaning.* Boston: Beacon Press.

Gardner, H. E. (2011). *Frames of mind: The theory of multiple intelligences.* New York: Basic Books.

Garvick, S., Peacock, B., & Gillette, C. (2022). COVID-19 and physician assistant faculty burnout: A year into the pandemic. *Journal of Physician Assistant Education, 33*(2), 135–138.

Goldstein, K. (1995). *The organism.* Princeton, NJ: ZONE Books.

Harris, H. S., & Martin, E. W. (2012). Student motivations for choosing online classes. *International Journal for the Scholarship of Teaching and Learning, 6*(2), 1–8. https://eric.ed.gov/?id=EJ1135583.

Hernández, E. H., Lozano-Jiménez, J. E., de Roba Noguera, J. M., & Moreno-Murcia, J. A. (2022). Relationships among instructor autonomy support, and university students' learning approaches, perceived professional competence, and life satisfaction. *PLoS ONE, 17*(4), e0266039. https://doi.org/10.1371/journal.pone.0266039.

James, W. (1890). *Principles of psychology, vols. I, II.* New York: Henry Holt & Co.

Jang, H., Reeve, J., & Deci, E. (2010). Engaging students in learning activities: It is not autonomy support or structure but autonomy support and structure. *Journal of Educational Psychology, 102*(3), 588–600.

Jang, H., Reeve, J., & Halusic, M. (2016). A new autonomy-supportive way of teaching that increases conceptual learning: Teaching in students' preferred ways. *The Journal of Experimental Education, 84*(4), 686–701.

Jones, E. M. (1999). Carl Rogers and the IHM Nuns: Sensitivity training, psychological warfare, and the "Catholic problem." *Culture Wars,* October.

Knowles, M. (1989). *The making of an adult educator: An autobiographical journey.* San Francisco: Jossey-Bass.

Kohn, A. (2018). *Punished by rewards: The trouble with gold stars, incentives, A's, praise, and other bribes* (25th anniversary edition). San Francisco: HarperOne.

Loebach, J., Rakow, D. A., Meredith, G., & McCuskey Shepley, M. (2022). Time outdoors in nature to improve staff well-being: Examining changes in behaviors and motivations among university staff in the use of natural outdoor environments since the emergence of the COVID-19 pandemic. *Frontiers in Psychology, 13*. https://doi.org./10.3389/fp-syg.2022.869122.

Lozano-Jiménez, J. E., Huéscar, E., & Moreno-Murcia, J. A. (2021). From autonomy support and grit to satisfaction with life through self-determined motivation and group cohesion in higher education. *Frontiers in Psychology, 11*(579492), 1–10.

Ma, Y., Ma, C., & Lan, X. (2020). Uncovering the moderating role of grit and gender in the association between teacher autonomy support and social competence among Chinese undergraduate students. *International Journal of Environmental Research and Public Health, 17*(6398), 1–17. https://doi.org/10.3390/ijerph17176398.

Ma, Y., Ma, C., & Lan, X. (2022). A person-centered analysis of emotional-behavioral functioning profiles in adolescents: Associations with teacher autonomy support and growth mindset. *Current Psychology*. https://doi.org/10.1007/s1214402203163-2.

Maslow, A. (1943). A theory of human motivation. *Psychological Review, 50*, 370–396.

Matos, L., Reeve, J., Herrera, D., & Claux, M. (2018). Students' agentic engagement predicts longitudinal increases in perceived autonomy-supportive teaching: The squeaky wheel gets the grease. *The Journal of Experimental Education, 86*(4), 592–609.

McClain-Smith, T. (2017). *Using autonomy supportive teaching with nontraditional distance learners* [Unpublished doctoral dissertation]. Fort Lauderdale, FL: Nova Southeastern University.

Milton, J. (2002). *The road to malpsychia: Humanistic psychology and our discontents*. New York: Encounter Books.

Neufield, A., & Malin, G. (2020). How medical students' perceptions of instructor autonomy-support mediate their motivation and psychological well-being. *Medical Teacher, 42*(6), 650–656.

Neufield, A., & Malin, G. (2021). A commentary on autonomy-supportive teaching: A reply to Duguid et al. (2020). *Medical Teacher, 43*(2), 238–245.

Newport, C. (2012). *So good they can't ignore you: Why skills trump passion in the quest for work you love*. New York: Hachette.

Reed, M. (2013). *Confessions of a community college administrator*. San Francisco: Jossey-Bass.

Reeve, J. (2009). Why teachers adopt a controlling motivating style toward students and how they can become more autonomy supportive. *Educational Psychologist, 44*(3), 159–175.

Reeve, J. (2016). Autonomy-supportive teaching: What it is, how to do it. In W. C. Liu, J. C. K. Wang, & R. M. Ryan (Eds.), *Building autonomous learners: Perspectives from research and practice using self-determination theory* (pp. 129–152). Berlin: Springer.

Reeve, J., & Cheon, S. H. (2021). Autonomy-supportive teaching: Its malleability, benefits, and potential to improve educational practice. *Educational Psychologist, 57*(1), 54–77.

Reeve, J., Ryan, R. M., Cheon, S. H., Matos, L., & Kaplan, H. (2022). *Supporting students' motivation: Strategies for success*. Oxfordshire, UK: Routledge.

Reeve, J., Vansteenkiste, M., Assor, A., Ahmad, I., Cheon, S. H., Jang, H., Kaplan, H., Moss, J. D., Olaussen, B. S., & Wang, C. K. J. (2014). The beliefs that underlie autonomy-supportive and controlling teaching: A multinational investigation. *Motivation and Emotion, 38*(1), 93–110.

Rogers, C. R. (1961). *On becoming a person: A therapist's view of psychotherapy*. Boston: Houghton Mifflin.

Rogers, C. R. (1969). *Freedom to learn*. Indianapolis: Merrill.

Rogers, C. R. (1984). *Freedom to learn for the 80s*. Indianapolis: Merrill.

Rogers, C. R. (1995). *A way of being: The founder of the human potential movement looks back on a distinguished career*. New York: Harper Perennial.

Rogers, C. R., Lyon, H. C., & Tausch, R. (2014). *On becoming an effective teacher: Person-centered teaching, psychology, philosophy, and dialogues with Carl R. Rogers and Harold Lyon.* Oxfordshire, UK: Routledge.

Ryff, C. D., & Singer, B. H. (2008). Know thyself and become what you are: A eudaimonic approach to psychological well-being. *Journal of Happiness Studies, 9*(1), 13–39.

Ryan, R., & Deci, E. (2000). Self-determination theory and the facilitation of intrinsic motivation, social development, and well-being. *American Psychologist, 55*(1), 68–78.

Ryan, R., & Deci, E. (2017). *Self-determination theory: Basic psychological needs in motivation, development, and wellness.* New York: Guilford Press.

Salmela-Aro, K., Upadyaya, K., Ronkainen, I., & Hietajärvi, L. (2022). Study burnout and engagement during COVID-19 among university students: The role of demands, resources, and psychological needs. *Journal of Happiness Studies: An Interdisciplinary Forum on Subjective Well-being, 23*, 2685–2702.

Seligman, M. (1991). *Learned optimism: How to change your mind and your life.* New York: Alfred A. Knopf.

Skinner, B. F. (1958). Teaching machines. *Science, 128*(3330), 969–977.

Skinner, B. F. (1971). *Beyond freedom and dignity.* New York: Bantam Books.

Spauling, D. T. (2013). *Program evaluation in practice: Core concepts and examples for discussion and analysis.* San Francisco: Jossey-Bass.

Taylor, D. G., & Frechette, M. (2022). The impact of workload, productivity, and social support on burnout among marketing faculty during the COVID-19 pandemic. *Journal of Marketing Education, 44*(2), 134–148.

Tenenbaum, S. (1961). Student-centered teaching as experienced by a participant. In C. R. Rogers (Ed.), *On becoming a person: A therapist's view of psychotherapy* (pp. 297–313). Boston: Houghton Mifflin Co.

Thorndike, E. (1910). The contribution of psychology to education. *Journal of Educational Psychology, 1*, 5–12.

Toubasi, A. A., Hasuneh, M. M., Al Karmi, J. S., Haddad, T. A., & Kalbouneh, H. M. (2022). Burnout among university students during distance learning period due to the COVID-19 pandemic: A cross sectional study at the University of Jordan. *Int J Psychiatry Med.* doi: 10.1177/00912174221107780.

Turkle, S. (2011). *Alone together: Why we expect more from technology and less from each other.* New York: Basic Books.

Turkle, S. (2014). *Reclaiming conversation: The power of talk in a digital age.* London: Penguin Books.

Villarreal, M. L., & García, H. A. (2016). Self-determination and goal aspirations: African American and Latino males' perceptions of their persistence in community college basic and transfer-level writing courses. *Community College Journal of Research and Practice, 40*(10), 838–853.

Wang, C., Kayla Hsu, H., Bonem, E. M., Moss, J. D., Yu, S., Nelson, D. B., & Leveque-Bristol, C. (2019). Need satisfaction and need dissatisfaction: A comparative study of online and face-to-face learning contexts. *Computers in Human Behavior, 95*, 114–115.

Watson, J. B. (1930). *Behaviorism.* New York: W. W. Norton & Co.

Whitehead, A. N. (1929). *The aims of education.* New York: The Free Press.

Whitehead, P. (2016). *Psychologizing: A personal, practice-based approach to psychology.* Lanham, MD: Rowman & Littlefield.

Whitehead, P. (2017). Goldstein's self-actualization: A biosemiotic view. *The Humanistic Psychologist, 45*(1), 71–83.

Williams, G. C., Wiener, M. W., Markakis, K. M., Reeve, J., & Deci, E. L. (1994). Medical student motivation for internal medicine. *Journal of General Internal Medicine, 9*, 327–333.

Index

About the Author

Patrick M. Whitehead is associate professor of psychology and coordinator of general education at Albany State University, where he was named 2019 scholar of the year. He has published six books, including *Psychologizing: A Personal, Practice-based Approach to Psychology*, and dozens of articles in the fields of psychology, philosophy, and higher education. He lives on a farm in Albany, Georgia, USA, with his wife, Erica. For more information and resources for college faculty, see www.patrickmwhitehead.com.